ANTI-OCULUS

ANTI-OCULUS
A PHILOSOPHY OF ESCAPE

ACID HORIZON

Published by Repeater Books

An imprint of Watkins Media Ltd

Unit 11 Shepperton House

89-93 Shepperton Road

London

N1 3DF

United Kingdom

www.repeaterbooks.com

A Repeater Books paperback original 2023

1

Distributed in the United States by Random House, Inc., New York.

Copyright Acid Horizon © 2023

Acid Horizon assert the moral right to be identified as the authors of this work.

ISBN: 9781915672094

Ebook ISBN: 9781915672100

Printed and bound in the United Kingdom by TJ Books Limited

Dedicated to the memory of Austin Blackburn Wiles, a friend who taught us the art of philosophical autopsy.

CONTENTS

INTRODUCTION

This manual provides a cybernetic analysis of the machinations of control. Cybernetics is the interdisciplinary science of control and communication. One can use cybernetics as a science to build social machines of control, and one can use cybernetics to analyze the machinations of production that attempt to direct and govern social reality. Social machines exist, but the schema of a social machine is always abstract in the form of a diagram of relations between its material and the functions it is to take on in being inserted into such a machine. For example, one can make a diagram of a factory and its various power relations between workers and bosses, distributed according to each of their functions on the assembly line, and can build many such factories according to the machine. The diagram is a real relation *of power*, yet equally an abstract machine whose reality is established *by power*, and configured by the intersection between the histories of both power and the sciences of government which depend on it. Schemata of management do not come into actual operation by their own power, but by the power that actualizes them, a power which itself may be caught in, even addicted to, its own machinations. Such is the case with the dominant machine that cancerously only produces itself: *capital*.

We live within a planetary machine defined by the

production of capital and the management of life to ensure this machine's stability and endurance. Life is an undefinable expanse of possibilities. This cybernetic machine is one which functions to restrain and represent these possibilities in order to sell them back to you as a refined and neutralized product. The capitalist system is not, however, omniscient. The corrective measures it applies are predominantly derived from confrontations with that which aims to escape it. In any circuitry, there is resistance. This resistance always precedes the machines that work tirelessly to quell it. Capitalism organizes the world, but it always organizes *against* an alternative mode of living that is not immediately economic. It is not that there is simply "no alternative," but rather that capitalism sustains itself by identifying and then destroying or integrating threats to its stability. This progressive destruction of non-economic forms of life is not a sign of capitalism's various strengths, but rather its weaknesses.

Our aim is to present various machines of contemporary and historical control over life, imagination, and expression. It is not that these machines simply "don't work" or will inevitably fail. Cybernetics is a science of management that takes crisis as its milieu. Capitalism is always in crisis; cybernetics is the logistics of crisis. Cybernetics evacuates all politics in favor of management. We would venture to say it is the crystallization of the cynicism at the end of politics, masquerading as the end of history.

We recognize that we are arriving on an already bloodied scene. But the cybernetic hope of an escape from capital *was always a lie*. We cannot automate our way out of an automation that seeks to impose itself as a totality. The utopians demand we refrain from such a line of thought, with a promise that liberation lies on the other side of automation's invasion of every facet of life. Capital will not be tricked into producing a "red plenty." Such a view is a trickle-down transcendence of capitalism.

When we speak of the cybernetic, we do not mean only a particular set of information technologies — this is not a diatribe against phones or computers. If we single out a particular technology or methodology, this is only because it allows us to grasp what is fundamental to the cybernetic framework: the interplay between a representation of the world, its inhabitants, its movements, and, most crucially, *its policing*.

This book is a catalog of machines of control — be it the control of the body, the psyche, the self, or even the control of revolt against the system itself. In presenting these machines, we hope to provide a manual of escape. It is only through an intimate analysis of the machines of control that one can work to short-circuit them and reverse-engineer a way out.

We must note that the philosophy of escape is not *itself* escape. However, as the cyberneticists have understood well, any transformation of the world is predicated on a transformation of its conception. We do not seek a society without revolts, as that promises nothing but a continuation of the disaster. The disaster of history is the incessant pacification of all that resists. In fact, we have no interest in producing something that would only be a new program to police straying bodies, proliferate "proper" images of thought, or peddle updated categories of surveillable subjects. Philosophy, as we understand it, is the conceptual proliferation of theoretical weapons aimed at the order of things. Anything else is mere collaboration.

We will begin our elaboration of the cybernetics of the present through one of its most popular cultural images: the cyberpunk dystopia of "high tech, low life." The point of this is to illustrate how the social relations of cyberpunk are not ephemeral or fictional elements of a distant future, but are fully operational in the current situation. Following this, in the second chapter, we present the core elements of cybernetic theory — those of feedback and the homeostasis of systems through the ways in which revolts are contained. This is both a thermodynamics of political dissidence as well as a cybernetic theory of riot policing. The central question of this part of our investigation is a simple one: How bad does it have to get before things boil over into active revolt?

From here, we move from the streets to the embodied self and the machinations through which identity and expression are policed. The third chapter exemplifies our method of machinic explanations of social phenomena in order to make possible ways of reverse-engineering an escape. This chapter's mode of presentation is in the form of a fictional catalog provided by a cybernetic consultancy firm. Their purpose? To promote their analysis of the ways in which categories of identity, be they racial, medical, sexual, or otherwise, can be produced and policed. It is in this way that apparatuses such as racialization, ableism, transphobia, and the destruction of the political imagination will be presented as technologies of governance that must be understood in order to be neutralized. It is, loosely put, the eye of *Oculus* as it lays bare its violent means. Chapter four develops an account of "going astray" under this eye of power and the way in which technologies of the subject seek to eliminate or re-insert divergent subjectivities into a normalized productive society. It shines a proverbial light on the eugenic history of the management and correction of life. This chapter is at once a history of biopolitical modernity, that which resists its interventions, and a new account of anarchy that lies dormant in the ableist histories of psychiatry, penality, and philosophy. In the final chapter, we locate the epistemological channels of the escaping cybernetization of the psyche. The field of contestation is in the realm of the image, the imaginary, and the power to imagine otherwise.

THE CYBERPUNK PRESENT

The image of the future promised by cyberpunk was a vision of ecstasy and anxiety all at once. The cyberpunk image was equally a warning, an oncoming threat that was also already here. Cyberpunk prophesized a latent future that the neoliberal counter-revolution in the latter half of the twentieth century was already piloting us towards. The warning and promise of a future that has become our present can be found in the most cursory definition of cyberpunk: "High-tech, low life."

First, we have a clause that we will describe as "ecstatic." This is the promise of "high tech," i.e., that the human may escape its bodily confines into a machinic realm — be it a cyberspace of communication, or a replacement of the organic with the technical through implantation and bionic augmentation. Cyborg or Cyberia. In either case, there was a promise of an escape from the body as well as an extension thereof, an indifference to limits, and hence an escape from the limits of a biological system itself already regulated under various regimes. High-techstasy, the meat is coming out of itself. Sadie Plant describes the promise of the realm of communication:

> Cyberspace emerged as a disembodied zone wilder than the wildest West, racier than the space race, sexier than sex, even better than walking on the

7

moon. This was the final of final frontiers, the purest of virgin islands, the newest of new territories, a reality designed to human specifications, an artificial zone ripe for an infinite process of colonization, able to. satisfy every last desire, especially that to escape from "the meat."[1]

Secondly, we have the promise of "low life." "Low" here is not a quantitative measure, but a qualitative one. In cyberpunk dystopias, Life is often abundant — stacked together in cramped tenements and decrepit towers at extortionate rents. Life for the living often becomes a series of subscription services to vital medications and new forms of indentured servitude in maintenance of cybernetically regulated organs. Cyberpunk worlds proliferate new forms of machinic health and machinic sickness, and as such a characteristic of living in a cyberpunk time is a perpetual battle for healthcare against those who would regulate people out of it, and hence out of existence. That one could become a "cyborg" is not "low" in any fluffy humanist sense of violating the sacredness of the unity of Mankind, but rather what is "low" is that one must lower oneself to servitude in order to maintain one's parts. The cyborg is a being determined by a higher machine, that of perpetual debt. There is nonetheless a quantitative dimension to "low life": you interact with the living less (or rather, you interact with the living as if they were a machine), and the life is increasingly automated (or in the old term, *cybernated*) out of living. Interactions between service providers and users are increasingly mediated by online tools, which obscure the laborers behind them; the human element is diminished, and humans are reduced to their ability to generate input for the online machines. Sites for finding jobs, ordering essentials, consuming "content" (and generating precious data), and endless little luxuries call upon the user to identify themselves, to provide themselves with a name, a code. Each divides the subject into various "accounts" of themselves: within the individual sits a dividual of many accounts, through which it accounts for itself before the service provider. "My data feed the databases obediently. Amazon, Google, YouTube, WhatsApp, Samsung, Telegram know more about me than the state."[2]

We should not place the danger outside of the state, however. The proliferation of "accounts" also reintroduces imminent dangers from the state and the police. The creation of an account often comes with a variable degree of anonymity in terms of how much identifying data one is required to hand over to the machine. Here lies the inherent danger, and in many cases the dangerous actuality, of the reintroduction of the national border checkpoint into cyberspace. The introduction of the national border into cyberspace exists by virtue of the same governmental rationality that proliferates the cybernation (we prefer this old term for "automation") and communication revolution that is mass surveillance. Further — and as will be discussed in multiple places throughout this "text"; this toolkit of concepts, this imaginal-intellectual arsenal — these surveillance and analytical engines are themselves produced and made possible by those they oppress. This is especially the case with the refugee and the migrant, "the new underclass of silicon-age capitalism... the cheap and captive labor force — rightless, rootless, peripatetic and temporary, illegal even — without which post-industrial society cannot run."[3]

High-techstasy is co-extensive with the world-sprawling capitalist machine, further intensifying its gaze upon the world as a territory for even greater machines of accumulation and production; mapping the world for the resources it needs to achieve its goals. The cybernation and communication revolutions have extended our abilities to sense. We can hear a scream from miles away with a phone, we can use satellites to sense the whole planet. The eye of cyber-capital is a mapping eye, an eye which maps out the territory of experience that it extends to in order to divide it, diagrammatically, into forms of property and systems of capital accumulation and expansion. The Cyberpunk Present is an acceleration, a cybernation, of Empire. Cyber-capital, much like Empire, requires a human face, many in fact, and it tries to make its own face(s) yours too, so that you see through these faces alone.

Cyber-capital encloses and regulates the bounds of identity in trying to map out the user at the same time as it seeks to produce an identity equal to that of the mapping. The oldest and most active forms of these mappings, racialization and gender stratification, are hence built into the eye of Capital, which aims to analyze and map out everything, so as to make the best bets on its returns at the same time that it reduces the object of its gaze to an exchangeable commodity. Cyber-capital loves facial recognition, and facial recognition is nonetheless always embarrassing for it, because it gives its own game away as a racist and often transphobic form of digital phrenology. We will always see the accelerating, digital proliferation of gendered and racialized identification, which arrive on the scene when cyber-capital tries to analyze and categorize the face with its cybernetic eye. This eye, which we shall call the eye of *Ocularity*; *the*

Oculus, which has come into its own under Capitalist Hegemony. These borders regulate the obscured human element of cybernetic capitalism, the life that has been plunged into the deepest depths by what this book identifies as the "Cyberpunk Present" or "*Cybercene era*" (as opposed to "the Anthropocene").

Cyberpositive theorists in the late 90s and early 2000s once claimed that the cybernetic revolution would entail the end of domination. Domination was said to presuppose an external dominator, imposing its sovereignty from outside the immediate connections of everyday life and structuring it accordingly. Contrastingly, *control* was immanent to the system, built in, self-regulating — purely an expression of the actuality of its own conditions of possibility.[4] However, regardless of what seeming freedoms cybernetic regulation allowed for in daily life — which were more often than not freedoms of consumption — their scope was always already regulated in advance. Such regulation, as the history of capitalism and of the production of subjectivity entails, is nonetheless imposed by a sovereign tendency of social management that tends towards capital accumulation and extraction. There is always a boundary of coercion and domination within any free-flowing communicative space of control. Escape from the Cybercene hence presupposes an insurgent exposure of its dominating sovereign elements — the apparatuses of state and civil control, as Sivanandan took great strides to highlight:

> Civil society is no pure terrain of consent where hegemonies can play at will; it is ringed around, if not with coercion, with intimations of coercion — and that is enough to buttress the system's

hegemony. It is only in challenging state power that you expose the coercive face of the state to the people, sharpening their political sense and resistance, providing the temper and climate for "the construction" of more effective "social blocs." Conversely, you cannot take on the dominant hegemonies in civil society without at some point — at the point of effectiveness, in fact — falling foul of the system.[5]

The Cybercene is the dawn not of a new mode of power separate from domination or discipline, but rather the automation of domination as its disappearance into near invisibility — "control is nothing more than discipline effectuated at automated speeds."[6]

*

Of course, we are keeping the two elements of our definition of cyberpunk too separate here. There was at least a trade-off for machinic enslavement under megacorporations: *actual technology*. People who were born in the 90s somehow look back with nostalgia at the 1980s. They do so, tellingly, since 2008, when it became clear that the so-called "cool" parts of cyberpunk, the bionic arms and VR technology, were either rich-kid playthings or simply not happening. That is, unless you believed the bullshit spun by various tech-millionaires who all crumbled into exposing themselves as fascist nerds the very second interest rates *dared* to go beyond 0%, signaling that the era of virtually free money was over. Now enters the austerity of the Cyberpunk Present and its poverty, where "the prison is reimagined as wireless ankle monitors, the hospital as health tracking apps, and the school as endless online classes"[7] (for those in the imperial core at least, where consuming is often as much of a socially necessary function as laboring itself). Life is low, cheap, and yet the "high-tech" never really arrived, never trickled down. But at the very least the *image* could be communicated to us. The future-image of cyberpunk is constantly being fed to us through nostalgic media, speculative fiction, and the mass wallet-inspections that take place when Silicon Valley counter-insurgents scam their believers into investing in crypto or Martian fantasies. They didn't need to sell you a ticket off-world, they simply needed you to invest in the image of its possibility.

The Marxist tendency of the rate of profit to fall is one that we could easily say is accompanied in the Cyberpunk Present by a *tendency of the rate of prophecy to fail*. The ecstatic images of off-world utopias and cybernetic immortality are shown as extractive quackery, as mere images to generate investment. The higher the rate of failing prophecies, the more frantic the cyber-prophets begin to get in the face of the tide of "low-life" that awaits their followers. One begins at the ecstatic dawn of the image of high-tech, becomes anxious at its impossibility, and then pings back into the delusional ecstasies of faith in the new cyber-prophecies (or maybe you're worried, like so many in Silicon Valley, that an AI-God will punish you in the future if you don't help it to be born). Communication, mediation, image, and desire in the Cyberpunk Present: areas from which we offer, to the best of our collective abilities, hope for escape.

High tech, low life. These two clauses become integrated in the fact that the *Cybercene is the era where the management of life is at its highest intensity, for it is at its most technological.* Before *Oculus*, Life is not meant to be lived, but channeled, piloted, managed. The Cybercene established many pathways for a life, in order to maintain control over each path. It constitutes via regulation, and it regulates the ways in which you constitute yourself. The regulation of the body and its behavior is how life is directed in the Cybercene: *Oculus* sees like a doctor, a eugenicist, a drill sergeant, a psychiatrist, and a policeman in one (and through many devices). The aim is to keep the body on the paths mapped out for it in advance, never to engage in *going astray*. To flee whilst going astray is to create bonds of comradeship and imperceptibility, hiding from sight or within plain sight, and engaging in conspiracy to revolt. It is in conspiring with each other, in finding each other, that we will begin the process of short-circuiting the new networks of Imperialism, which we may destitute the Empire, and we can burn the whole fucking thing down. With this, we will begin.

BURN YOUR WAY OUT: THE CYBERNETICS OF REVOLT

What are the core components of Cybernetic Governance? How intense does the political situation have to get before things boil over? By what strategies does Cybernetic Government manage the heat of the people's rage at their material conditions of indignity? How do we short-circuit cybernetic society? How do we fry the circuits of control?

Sacrifice is heat, in which the intimacy of those who make up the system of common works is rediscovered. Violence is its principle, but the works limit it in time and space; it is subordinated to the concern for uniting and preserving the commonality.
          Georges Bataille, *The Accursed Share, Volume 1*[1]

I. BOILING OVER: SYSTEMS AND CYBERNATION

It is puzzling why an event where public anger spills over — becoming explosive social rage, reconfiguring the poles of "state" and "citizenry" into opposed forces of an active civil war — is so often described as a "boiling point." Although, maybe such puzzlement is more of a historical, technical, and cybernetic fact

A burning building during the George Floyd Insurrection, Minneapolis, 2020.

than an abstract or linguistic one. What we usually describe as a "boiling point" in everyday usage, in a household kettle or heating water on a stove, is hardly dangerous in and of itself. This is because reaching of a boiling point is not yet a boiling-over. The heat we generate poses little threat or disruption to the workings of the household and its appliances, so long as there is an act of intervention; a management of the heated matter that neutralizes its destructive potential. Such an intervention must be made before control over the energized flows, before the bubbling violence of the body of water, is lost.

Now *there* is the danger, in that moment of intervention or just preceding it. It is in the moment where an intervention risks failure either by a failing to intervene to the proper degree or by failing to intervene and control the heat at the proper time. Such a failure is a failure of control, a failure to manage the intensities of heat and the body of water this heat excites and partially evaporates. What is lost in the factor of evaporation is a minor cost for the utility of what remains, the loss of water in steam is usually negligible for the ends of the one doing the boiling. In fact, often the loss is part of the whole process, part of the body is *sacrificed* so that heat may be contained at a stable and controllable level. Sacrifice occurs for sake of the utility as well as the unity of the process (because if all goes well, nothing boils over, nothing gets destroyed or damaged, and all the components can be used again).

In such processes, things usually run smoothly when given proper attention — as long as one intervenes either at or before the *last* moment of boiling before the boiling-over. After this last moment, nothing can be done within the confines of the current operation, and there is in all likelihood a net loss of the usefulness of the water in terms of what one was aiming to do with it in heating it up. The last moment of control is really the penultimate moment before, ultimately, control has been lost. After this point, the forces which seek to re-establish control must contend with that which it wishes to control, in order to re-assert and re-impose itself. Control over the situation is understood to be (at least temporarily) lost and must be re-imposed, or the territory must be abandoned. Beyond this penultimate point, the water's function, what it does or can do, transforms, breaks away from the unity of its assigned function — from being an ingredient in, say, a cup of tea — towards becoming a mutilating flow of hot intensity that melts, scars, and deforms. What boils over may not only burn through the systems of its containment, but can equally damage the systems connected to it — potentially even scolding the forces that try to re-impose control, melting the master of the house.

This "last" or rather penultimate moment is the moment of the limit, when the marginal utility is zero, and after which marginal utility is negative. All this means is that, in terms of the system, what little benefit is produced is outweighed by the risk or danger generated in producing it. Beyond this point, what is ultimately produced serves no use but anti-use, anti-function, and anti-pleasure for those whom would extract it — the cost is too high, and so to get any use out of it, it's better not to go all at once, but to carefully navigate and to correct the course of operations away from a breaching of negative utility (the Greek κυβερνάω, *kybernáō*, meaning to steer or navigate, gives us our terms for cybernetics and cybernation). The "boiling point" is typically where we enter the zone where we begin to confront the limit, a penultimate time and territory before the crossing of the limit.

When we transgress the borders of the limit, of the penultimate, we therefore pass beyond the threshold — the border of the ultimate. It is here where ultimately the body of water becomes insurgent — surges up from within, *rises up* from within the grasp of that which tries to control it — in the face of a weakened or lost control. The limit of a system is the penultimate state it can reach where functional organization is maintained. Beyond that is the point of the ultimate, where the system is past the threshold of stability and its organizational structure succumbs to an inevitable disruption.[2] If you do not want to transgress the limit in crossing the threshold of the ultimate, one must stop the process that pushes the body past this limit. One must suspend the operation, at least partially, in order to allow for it to begin again, in order to preserve its functionality from uncontrolled damage, and to reproduce this functionality for what it really is; its social purpose (the boiling of water for food preparation, sterilization, etc.).

The functionality of many an electric kettle is maintained by a mechanism that receives heat up until the limit of the point of boiling, and having received the quantitative heat-data corresponding to the heat-limit disengages the heating element. This is typically achieved by use of a bi-metallic strip, one that bends at the designated temperature point, breaking the circuit that powers the heating element and its continued heat generation. If this circuit breaker fails in its regulation, burn-out or explosive tension ensues, or at least the threat thereof invokes *panic*, and panic is a noisy gesture that clouds the judgment of management when something doesn't fit the program.[3] As Tiqqun conclude:

> Disabling the process of cybernetization, toppling the Empire, will require an opening to panic... Empire is a set of apparatuses aimed at forestalling and precluding the event, a process of control and rationalization.[4]

Great triumphs of electronics, physics, and material science have condensed themselves into this quantitative knowledge of the limit that has been imparted into the circuit-breaker function of that mechanism, making it into an automatic, self-regulating system of heat-management. Through the knowledge of the bi-metallic strip, the system solves its own problem of information as to when to turn off the heat before things shift from minimal risk to *absolute* risk, i.e., the uncertainty and unpredictability of when and to what degree things are getting destructive. This is not to say that, before the kettle-mechanism, all was simply guesswork; a tradition of knowledge concerning the rhythms of producing (that hardly needs such an abstract intervention) existed and continues to exist in the continuity of millions of households. The sensor, the one who watches the boil, has been simply integrated into the appliance.

The problematic of management here is solidifying the knowledge of where to intervene on behalf of the forces that seek to impose a system of management upon a given material. It is about solving the problem of information, of knowing and predicting how a body behaves in relation to its position within the system in which it has been enclosed; a body of water being managed so that it simply boils within the kettle or pan rather than overflowing, melting, scolding, etc.

This problematic and the question of its solution(s) characterizes the theoretical and technical shift that is *cybernetics*: the science of control systems dependent on information or feedback received by mechanisms of management and intervention upon the behavior of a body within such a system.[5] Systems dependent on feedback, or "feedback systems," are based on closure and enclosure; they are non-linear and rely on the looping or feeding-back of information from previous happenings. As one of the prophets of systems theory, Jay W. Forrester, describes such systems:

> A feedback system, which is sometimes called a "closed" system, is influenced by its own past behavior. A feedback system has a closed loop structure which brings results from past action of the system back to control future action. One class of system — negative feedback — seeks a goal and responds as a consequence of failing to achieve that goal. A second class of system — positive feedback — generates growth processes wherein action builds a result that generates greater action.
>
> A feedback system controls action based on the results from previous action.[6]

Cybernetics seems to have always had a fascination with the management of heat, as suggested by its *ur*-examples of cybernetic machines — most notably the thermostat, used as examples by both Forrester[7] and the popularizer of the science Norbert Wiener.[8] Again, Forrester:

The heating system of a house is controlled by a thermostat which responds to the heat previously produced by the furnace. Because the heat already produced by the system controls the forthcoming generation of heat, the heating system represents a negative feedback system that seeks the goal of proper temperature.[9]

Such a process characteristically operates via negative feedback. "Feedback," because it operates in a relatively closed loop in which previously generated heat informs levels of future generation, and "negative" because it works against the direction of additional heat-generation insofar as this addition tends towards the quantitative limit of the system's control and productive utility.[10] Beyond that, things overheat beyond viability and control must be re-imposed. We wouldn't want the whole system burning down, of course. Previous cyberneticists thought that positive feedback would achieve this and advocated for an acceleration of the process, a relaxing of control so that the system would achieve its own emancipation and self-dissolution — spiraling out into a post-human "Outside" of cybernetic nomadism.[11] This thesis was, at best, overly optimistic.

II. THE THERMOSTATIC HYPOTHESIS

The model of control presented here is *thermostatic*. Thermostasis is the maintenance of a certain desired temperature by the regulation of heat flows through a body, e.g., the body of water within a radiator or a furnace. This control aims at the proper rhythm, and feedback allows for modifications to be made, such that things run in the proper order. Regulate the heat, discover the limit (trial and error are always good systems of feedback for the designer and engineer of control). Stay within the limit or just before its penultimate boundary, and the whole system should keep working for its intended function. The system lives another day to begin again.

Yet cybernetics — as evidenced by the explosion of information technology into our everyday lives, be it social media systems of feedback, which target us for advertising and sell our responses as commodified data, or cashless payment systems, which allow for the tracking of our movements and the desirability of our destinations — is far from a separate sphere of number-crunching. It is not simply a detached study of existing systems, but projects systemic unity onto existing social spheres of production and interaction in order to develop processes of regulation which keep them stable. The realm of cybernetics is not merely "a virtual space that would be superimposed on the real world. It has become clear that cybernetics is rather *an autonomous world of apparatuses merged with the capitalist project insofar as the latter is a political project.*"[12]

Cybernetics carries an in-built and inextricable idea of the human as a system of self-regulating inputs and outputs in relatively closed systems and proudly declares this to be the case: "The idea of man as a sort of machine-like system and the resemblances between human nervous systems and computers led to the science of cybernetics — the science of control and communication."[13] Societies, zones that are governed, as well as the persona within them and their bodies, are considered as machines that can be regulated, harmonized, and perfected in their integration into wider networks of production. These networks of production are themselves machinic or mega-machinic. The "machine" here in the cybernetic view of things stands in for any purposive system,[14] i.e., any system that is purposive in working towards the production of a certain kind of output from an input by way of mechanisms, which regulate production towards such a purpose.

This process of integration — accelerated and intensified in its proliferation under neoliberal or cybernetic capitalism — is what Deleuze and Guattari call "*machinic enslavement*," which exists when "human beings themselves are constituent pieces of a machine that they compose among themselves and with other things (animal, tools), under the control and direction of a higher unity," the unity of a state or governing system considered or enclosed as a self-relating loop or whole.[15] Populations, persons, and bodies in movement are, in the cybernetic worldview, to be directed in their resistance as well as in their compliance to maintain unified stability and to provide feedback for reinforcement of the mega-machinic function. Unity itself can provide for the very subjectivity of those human beings within such a system, in the production of a subjectivity, "when the higher unity constitutes the human being as a subject linked to a new exterior object, which can be an animal, a tool, or even a machine."[16] Identifying with a system or subsystem integrates compliance into the whole or manages it within an ocular schema (see the manual recovered from the cyberneticists at I.R.I.S., provided in this book). In this mode, one is not a part of the machine of, say, advertisement and marketing coupled with consumption, but rather one is a user of a phone, a fan of X brand, and integrates this into their identity, and the practice of this identity/identification motivates consumption, which feeds back into informational capture — into which the subject itself is integrated at the same time that it is produced and captured.

Electoral polling functions in the exact same manner, and all of these means of enjoyment and controlled expression channel the heat of desire as well as discontent, allowing us (and the system) to let off a little steam. It is here where the thermostatic hypothesis exceeds the machine that has been our previous model: the kettle. The kettle relies upon letting off steam as a kind of sacrifice of the water for the sake of the whole system. However, our most brilliant cyberneticists have re-integrated the letting-off of steam into a mode of productivity and systemic reinforcement. With great fury at the system, one can blow off some steam in anti-capitalist "retail therapy," if one buys the Che Guevara T-shirt. One can vote for a nominally social-democratic party, such as the British Labour Party, which promises only to restore apparatuses such as the police and the border-camp regime to their properly managed and adequately funded functionality. Under thermostatic governance, the best kind of steam to let off is that which is let off without sacrifice. In the electoral sphere and the sphere of cultural commodity consumption, this has been achieved to the level of recuperation. Recuperation isn't a total neutralization, however. To return to a crass Bolshevik refrain — that the capitalist would *sell* you the rope is their folly, not the revolutionary who would buy it.

All this is to say that the kettle is but one abstract machine of thermostatic — and therefore cybernetic — government. On the level of the governance of

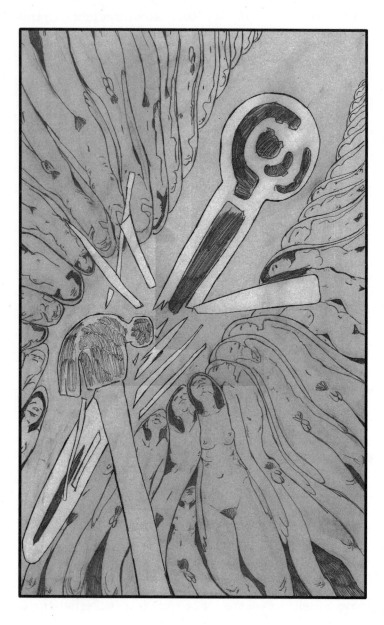

populations, we have always been thermostatic in how we have been governed. Or, at the very least, it serves as a regulative ideal to which governments tend to strive. The perfect, self-regulating system of political equilibrium is the idea that regulates the practice of system-building and system-correcting, absorbing feedback and information, orienting it towards the possibility of practically perfecting systemic action in a quasi-Kantian manner.[17] This tendency towards perfection motivates administrations or their theoretical resources — which may nonetheless go unheeded by governments used to stability and impunity — towards the ideal of perfect management. This is quasi-Kantian because, whilst Kant's regulative ideals were ideas of practical principles and inferences from them, which regulated intellectual and practical conduct, they neither referred to nor constituted any real object of possible experience. Few cyberneticists would affirm the ability to perfect a system of information and management, but in the desire to capture more and more data, they would nonetheless act *as if* such perfection or minimalization of all imperfection was an immanent reality ("all we need is more data, there's nothing we won't be able to solve").

This ideal of perfect management ironically reached its scientific height of popularity in the post-war era; cybernetic self-regulation is "a theory of equilibrium originating in a context of crisis."[18] The heat that passes through the social body is managed down to an approximation of the *last* or penultimate body that can be sacrificed before they risk unpredictable eruption, before their control becomes uncertain, unpredictable. During pandemics, what is managed is often the heat of deathly or debilitating feverishness. This heat is channeled and redistributed in rhythmic waves targeting marginal points of the social body as it is in all our examples: the racialized, the precariat, the impoverished, and the disabled. We see this again in the punishment and social murder of cost-of-living crises, where the poorest are made to choose between heating their homes and preserving their own vital warmth in feeding themselves or their children. Heating or eating — management of starvation or hypothermia, rather than its elimination. That is what governments bet on: "acceptable levels" of discontent — social murder.

During our climate crises, all we are doing is managing the heated bodies. For example, Fortress Europe manages those fleeing inhospitable zones of climate destitution at the same time as it repels those fleeing the heat of war — at least, those not favored by white-supremacist border policies or geopolitical preference (which are often the same thing). How does it manage them? Neocolonial concentration camps for "processing" on the one hand, and the cultivation of the Mediterranean as the world's largest mass grave on the other. In war, one either fights to the *last*, penultimate fighting force, before the war machine collapses into something else entirely, or it is fought until ultimately one side cannot fight anymore, and an active war machine is either annihilated or reduced to a dormant faculty of the state, i.e., the military institution (which may not exhaust the war machine, to speak of underground resistances and guerrilla insurgencies).

Think of the heatwaves at the margins of survivability across the world: in India, China, even in the United Kingdom (an archipelago currently swimming in its own fecal matter, adept at managing and channeling discontent through perpetual culture-war). What is managed is the heat that threatens economic productivity on the one hand (hence similar measures to a pandemic in terms of working from home for office workers, etc.), and the heat that rips through the marginalized bodies on the other. Biopolitics for productive life; necropolitics for life designated unworthy of saving. This is the model of sovereignty of the thermostatic or cybernetic hypothesis, and as Achille Mbembe writes, the power to "kill or to let live thus constitutes sovereignty's limits, its principal attributes. To be sovereign is to exert one's control over mortality and to define life as the deployment and manifestation of power."[19]

This is a necropolitics that manages the sacrifice of parts of a social body, or bodies within an assemblage of bodies, which we would call a socio-economic network. Typically, this covers the bodies of persons within it as well as the bodies of infrastructure, of systems and dynamics of care and community. The management is as intrinsic to the function of the whole as the loss that is steam from a kettle, or rather, these systems themselves present this intrinsic loss as absolutely necessary for the preservation of the social order. The management of both life and death is united in the thermostatic maintenance of the "house" of these systems. This is *their* domain, the region in which the house-management, the literal *oikonomia* (the theological term from which we receive "economy," the *nomos* or ruling of the house and its affairs[20]) is practiced.

III. THE DAWNING INSURRECTION

The Government-Economy assemblage is turning up the heat, across all of its nodes, albeit to varying degrees — but nonetheless, most certainly. Planet-wide paradigms of governmentality coincide with planetary heating at both poles. Within a meticulously managed level of death and destitution in the functioning and reproduction of the dominant order, the *limit* of sacrifice is built into the bio/necropolitical regulation of a state-managed population, i.e., of a *policed one*. Yet the police are trained to be vehicles of coercive violence, and often operate with a violence in excess of their official duties in order to strengthen fear in the populations whom they deter from challenging them. Law does not prohibit illegality, but distributes it between various elements of society and at varying levels of punishment (if any). This is evident in, for example, the racial and class disparities of drug prosecutions. However, this is also the case with the distribution of violence, as exemplified by the impunity with which government operatives conduct eugenic campaigns of mass COVID death at the same time as they collaborate with the press to proliferate transphobic genocide. What is interesting is how our enemies are now so indulgent in their impunity that they may soon push populations beyond the boiling point.

The bi-metallic strip of government nonetheless aims to know at what time to bend, to trigger the kill-switch. The system has a kind of metastable aim, or at least likes to think it does, and so it will occasionally let another element take over, to steer the ship with a safe, neutralized oppositional force (such is the fate of all social-democratic parties). It aims to know when to give some concessions — snap elections, reforms, representational semblances of solidarity and false promises — or redirections of heat — scapegoating, nationalism, terrorizing the population, and putting fires out sporadically — to keep the heat off of them, either to avoid boiling over or to catch the overflow into a neat receptacle where it can cool down. The last or penultimate human that the enemy can murder, however, is always anonymous to them at first. Their personality is not informative to these systems until it is too late and they become emblazoned upon the banners of a movement or a revolt.

Social data collection, opinion polls, etc., are not omniscient (and they could hardly ask in such direct terms whether people enjoy their economic death-machines). The *ultimate* case, especially if it is a person, has a name or names, and these names define a territory of struggle, which they ignite as the points of boiling-over into revolt; first national and then global. The *ultimate* human, the last person to be murdered by a system which triggers an acceleration into active revolt, is an entity that power struggles to quantitatively define. Systems of information-regulation only pick them up when it is too late: George Floyd, Breonna Taylor, Rodney King, Mark Duggan, Mahsa Amini, Brianna Ghey (to name but a few). These were the *ultimates*, the final bodies coated in hot blood before the heat crossed the threshold and the system could not simply "rebegin" without an entirely new operation, through which control is re-imposed on a territory — a territory that is now in active, burning revolt. The most iconic images of the George Floyd insurrections of 2020 were those of heat spilling over from the guns of the police and the images of their temples of murderous, sacrificial regulation being set ablaze. There is so much to learn from this event, provided that we refuse the counter-insurgent urge to denounce it or understate its intensity. As Idris Robinson teaches us:

> We all saw it. We all saw what happened after the murder of George Floyd. What occurred was an extremely violent and destructive rebellion. It was a phenomenon the likes of which we have not seen in America in 40 or 50 years. Very few of us have experienced anything of this magnitude: a precinct was immediately torched in Minneapolis, after which entire cities went up in flames — New York, Atlanta, Oakland, Seattle. Comparisons were quickly made with the riots after Martin Luther King's assassination. However, I think that we've gone further in this case, that 2020 went harder than 1968, and we're not even done yet.
>
> ... The fact is, whatever data or graphs they draw up, nothing will erase the fact that police cars were on fire in dozens of American cities.[21]

The ultimates cannot be sacrificed, only killed by an omnipresent state violence. In this sense, maybe we could call them *Homo Sacer*, because they cannot even become sacrifices, because sacrifice, like steam, is a function of preserving the unity of the whole operation. This is why, when Senator Pelosi thanked George Floyd "for sacrificing your life for justice,"[22] we all rightfully wretched, as if his death were for the sake of a self-corrective awakening of the American system and the distribution of its inherent violence. When one tries to make an ultimate into a sacrifice, one makes them into a *last,* and in doing so, power tries to reassure itself that it never had to *regain* control, but rather that everything was, and always has been, *under control*. These people were never sacrifices, they were ultimates; not the penultimate straw, but the straw that broke the proverbially cybernetic camel's back. Ultimately, the population knew that they had to spill out onto the streets and things needed to fucking burn. The state knew this too, but by then it was too late. Controlled revolt, managed opposition, can be regulatory mechanisms, but to insist that these are commonly the case risks giving the enemy too much credit, bordering on omniscience.

It is in the interest of the thermostatic regulation of populations to keep the dead nameless. Who is the last person who has to die of COVID, of heat exhaustion or heat stroke in India, of drowning in the Mediterranean Sea? By Russian bombs in Ukraine and Syria? By British arms in Yemen? By Israeli and American (we could add the "American" qualifier to so many more) arms in Palestine? At what limit is the point beyond which the subject of the state as citizen turns into the rioter and the revolutionary? We do not know this nor whether it could *ultimately* be known to any precise determination. As such, we can say that the state only has a rough idea, and the line between the limit/last and the ultimate is ambiguous. The last meal, the last eviction, the last bill, the last imprisonment, the last injury, the last promise broken, or the last deportation. From the state of things, it seems that the quantities in which we would enter the zone of the limit-case are incredibly high. This is particularly the case in areas where unions of marginalized bodies do not form where they would generate feedback loops of their own heat, unaware of the thermostatic regulation from above. It is here that they could turn up the heat on pockets of governmentality so as to accelerate that over-intensification towards the ultimate moment, where discontent morphs into destituency — into *de-institutionalization*, the breaking of the rigidity of a system and its self-reproduction. This means a total withdrawal from cybernetic sovereignty and its enclosed systems with their various subsystems and nodes, which compromise institutions at various scales across a social order that maintains social stability. As Saul Newman articulates it, the "de-institutionalization" or "destituent moment" is

> a withdrawal of support from the sovereign political order, without the desire to replace it with another sovereign political order. Sovereignty is instead suspended, deposed, de-instituted.[23]

Accelerationism, if it could be anything other than the trivial tactic that intensifies resistance to capital or intensifies tendencies in capital that capital cannot control, must become destitutional. It must become bottom-up, rather than technocratic. Capital will not simply be duped by technocratic promises of post-scarcity, for it sells post-scarcity dreams in order to create new frontiers of artificial scarcity for the sake of profit. As Sivanandan reminds us, the point "is to overthrow capitalism, not to join it in order to lead it astray into socialism."[24] The point is to render the circuits of capitalist control and accumulation inoperative. What is to be accelerated is the proliferation of spaces of non-control, which de-activates circuits and mechanisms of regulation and disrupts the rhythms by which they recuperate from attack. No firebreaks from the control room can be allowed. It must be the destituent communism, for it must, in its activity and heat-intensity, be that which Marx and Engels described before their capitulation and co-option:

> Communism is for us not a *state of affairs* which is to be established, an *ideal* to which reality [will] have to adjust itself. We call communism the *real* movement which abolishes the present state of things. The conditions of this movement result from the now existing premise.[25]

It must be the movement that turns up the heat on the master's house until — to put it in a particularly British turn of phrase — royalty really learns how to fucking sweat. Sweating is itself a homeostatic mechanism, of course, and a further brilliant example of the utility of the system, and so, when it comes to thermostasis itself, it's advisable to keep a cool head about it. That is, at least until thermostatic regulation of the economy rears its head as mastery and self-reproduction at the expense of the marginalized. At those points, clusters of heat and intensity would have to band together, move with nameless fluidity, and overspill with an insurgent burst of revolt worthy of a new Earth, radiating a new light over an emancipated territory, with tatters of the old circuitry festering in the heat.

IV. PRECARITY AND POLICING THE MOVEMENT

Banding together has become more difficult in certain regions due to precariousness in work and in domestic conditions. In cities and large towns, people move often due to gentrification, rent hikes, and wages not rising in line with inflation, causing a real loss. Hence, when the cyberneticist and NATO consultant F.H. George once predicted that "we will change our community life, moving away from isolated private houses to something more like interrelated networks of motels; this suggests a new type of community",[26] we can say that he was accurate yet optimistic. In fact, he was far too optimistic, given that these new communities of working people in economic circulation would have their motion in society defined by their precariousness, and by the fear of poverty and persecution that propels them into motion so that they could accumulate what little wealth was on offer to keep their lives stable.

Cybernetic governance needs to keep its subjects and machinic parts moving, not just in any direction, but in the direction pre-determined by pathways of control. The parts are set in motion and pre-directed within a circuit of economic productivity, such that they move in a way coherent with the system of production. These motions through the circuits are productive when they produce feedback (looking at ads, purchasing, marking their presence at ticket gates, etc.), and this feedback is commodified as data, which aids future regulation and generates further profit. Feedback is data; data is one of the paradigmatic commodities of the cybernetic-capitalist era. Movement throughout the circuitries of capitalism is what produces it, and this movement must be maintained according to the ideal tendency towards perfect governance and control. Discipline is not absent from cybernetic capitalism, not at all, but rather control compensates for archaic forms of discipline where it has become unproductive or detrimental to profit, and these new forms of control are marketed to us as new freedoms. This is the "freedom" of the highway and the "freedom" of travel across predetermined paths of access shaped by regulation and the historical bounds of private property. As Deleuze put it:

> You do not confine people with a highway. But by making highways, you multiply the means of control. I am not saying this is the only aim of highways, but people can travel infinitely and "freely" without being confined while being perfectly controlled. This is our future.[27]

Speaking today, we can say that this state of control is now the present for the "lucky ones" in controlled circumstances of neoliberal normality. To be a "lucky one" is just to be within the imperial core with a social productivity that relies on your constant consumption and enjoyment, which produces feedback-data for speculation and further investment. It is in this sense that capitalization can occur with enjoyment, but entirely without happiness. A peace treaty within our Cyberpunk Present consists in a significant portion of the working and lower-middle classes accepting this deal of control-feedback for consumption-enjoyment: a treaty for treats. As a simultaneously economic and ecological crisis kicks social mobility into reverse, we believe that this peace is currently unfolding itself as little more than a ceasefire. It is a matter of cultivating insurgent movements to rise to this challenge.

Containment is either a means of control in the first-order, or a second-order means of controlling the loss of control. Abnormal or insurgent forms of movement must therefore be contained, cordoned off. When things boil over, heat must not be allowed to gain momentum and accumulate, but must be surrounded, enclosed. In doing so, control mechanisms can then gradually regulate the heat of the insurgent or riotous body, letting it be gradually diminished in slow releases, or stamped out entirely like the lit match of a Guy Fawkes figure upon being apprehended.

When it comes to protests, this strategy is aptly named "containment" or "*kettling*."[28] Kettling represents an inversion of the traditional logics of anti-protest policing since the mid-1980s; "instead of rapidly diffusing the protest, it sets up a bounded space for containing and potentially absorbing its energy."[29] The kettle is a response to decentralized disruptive forms of protest, which seek to create blockages in places where productive motion typically occurs (streets, highways, etc.). The function of the kettle is to keep politically heated bodies from spreading out throughout the circuits and pathways and overloading them. The kettle contains protestors in order to create "zones of relative immobility to protect those urban circulations deemed productive."[30] In this, every policing of a protest reduces the police officer to a traffic cop.[31] The kettling agents, the traffic cops, direct flows of productive activity around the containment zone, creating a zone of exception within its boundaries. They aim at producing an internal outside to the zone of control, which is itself controlled: "the geared up bodies of the police, crowd control fencing or steel barricades are used, but also flexible and lightweight shutoff devices made of plastic fabric," creating internal walls within the city itself.[32]

The sides of this kettle then begin to function in

terms of their absolute deprivation of the forms of recognition or responsiveness to the bodies inside. This unresponsiveness is targeted at the biology of those inside: access to toilets, nutrition, medicine, heat itself may be refused.[33] "Kettling" is an ironic name given the inversion of its function as we have been considering it, although the principles of containment and control themselves have not changed. Rather than generating heat and regulating this through steam-release and the eventual ceasing of heat-generation at a certain point, the police kettle generates only coldness, and releases "cooled-down" protestors in small numbers gradually. It is centered around a politics of deceleration and intense, negative feedback in that it attempts to work against the direction of any boiling-over whatsoever.

Peter Waddington, the architect of the strategy as it was formulated in the UK, said as much:

The whole point was to slow everything down, to reduce the temperature, to calm down all parties, including the police. Because when you get people running around their nervous system switches from flight to fight, and [...] that's a recipe for them being aggressive and responsive. It struck me that using baton charges and things of that sort was just a recipe for putting officers under a sort of stress that would cause them to possibly use excessive force. So, the whole idea was slow things down, just encircle people, not allow them out of the kettle, except under controlled conditions and avoid situations of aggression or violence. And if it came from anyone, it would have to come from the protesters. The police would be in a defensive posture having established a cordon.[34]

This is not to say that there are no other intensities or kinds of heat generated within a space that is contained or kettled. In many ways, the police turn up the heat by provoking the panic that comes with being indefinitely trapped in the cold by an unresponsive force. Fires can even break out in kettles, but distinctly for reasons of enduring this indefinite detention. As a once-kettled friend relayed to me:

> Besides from the panic and the freezing cold, I couldn't help but think how all of us (there must have been about 2,000 of us kettled) were in a slow process of deterritorialization; we were being cooled off so as to be released into a different territory. I actually remember after being let out a policeman telling me and my friend that now we've "cooled off" we can "go home." What's also interesting is that concentrating the heat like that caused literal fires within the kettle. People set fire to a bus stop (as well as anything else flammable) and so the smell of burning plastic soaked the air.

The containment, of course, means that the ones getting burnt-out are the protestors themselves. The response to this tactic has therefore predominantly been one of motion and feedback from the protestors, creating lines of communication to avoid kettles via GPS, social media, etc., even to the extent that the police themselves become surrounded.[35]

This tactic of keeping people "running on the spot" is not, of course, solely applied in policing protests. Cyber-capital equally relies upon displacing and enclosing people so that they can constantly produce the data and feedback that reinforces this very system. This is exemplified in the case of the refugee-industrial complex, where refugees in camps are paid pennies for assigned tasks or "micro work," generating data to help systems of AI recognize the faces and linguistic mannerisms of people much like themselves through platforms like Amazon's Mechanical Turk.[36] Deportation, dispossession via war, and xenophobia all work in the service of population management that exploit poverty and precarity so long as solidarity with the other is minimized and they are made ever distant in the consciousness of the wider populace.

However, movements have responded in kind to both kettling and the racist forces of displacement. The kettling of the police themselves has already been mentioned, but a beautifully concrete example exists in the resistance to deportation vans in the United Kingdom. The police and the vans become blocked, encircled, charges are pushed back, until they give up and the empty vans leave with them. Decentralized networks of anti-raid groups spread information throughout communities, who break their participation in everyday circulation and swarm around the agents of deportation. Solidarity is heat, and nothing melts ICE quite like it.[37]

V. COMMUNIZATION AND COMMUNITY

Solidarity turns up the heat on the Thermostatic State and its movements of coercion. Movements of heat in revolt would have to assemble as accumulated points of resistance to such movement and coercive force — from jamming circuits of population management by blocking deportation vans until they leave empty, to undermining the material basis of precarity by distributing those labors that keep us alive and reproduce ourselves to live another day. For example (and this is but one example), by breaking them out of the units of the family that are maintained by cultural mandate (i.e., the nuclear family as the model of kinship) and founded upon gendered oppression and the historical dispossession of women, which forced them into unpaid domestic labor and the labor of the family.[38] To lay out the dynamic of reproductive labor at its most explicit:

> Capitalism does not value labor which keeps people living and ready for work (cooking, cleaning, caring, childbirth).
> But without this reproductive labor, capitalism would have no workers.
> By collectively organizing reproductive labor, we can refuse to work for the maintenance of capitalism.
> We can build a world where there is more to life than making more workers.[39]

The communization of reproductive labor detaches us from the material need that pulls us into the circuits through a sharing of care. It is the element of the commune, which also establishes its own detached loops where previously atomized knowledges can be shared amongst a new spirit of warmth, which must be fought for. Or, rather, these events and practices of detachment are no longer closed loops, but rather constant practices of short-circuiting, which overload habits and tendencies of control as they have been programmed into us, relating to how we have used our bodies in capitalist production. As M.E. O'Brien has articulated from the experience of communizing movements and occupations where control has been deactivated over a territory:

> When large numbers of people directly confront the state and capital in its forms that bring them into a shared location for multiple days, they often develop practices for collectively procuring food, cooking, and shared eating; for sleeping arrangements in proximity to each other; for sharing child rearing responsibilities and aiding disabled comrades. All work to share the work of care, to enable diverse participation, and to protect each other against harm.[40]

If there is to be one regulatory idea, let it not be as a cold ideal; an abstract essence of community to which we must statically be forced to conform, but rather the practice of coming together, with a new warmth that boils over into the circuitries.

Detach and deactivate in detaching, accumulate a new kind of collective intensity in order to create pockets of insurgent heat. Detach from a regulation that is dependent on you and the feedback your labor and motion generates, only to send such regulatory systems into meltdown when this energy is released back into these circuits, beyond their operational limits; into an ultimate confrontation where control loses itself as well as us. This is a short-circuiting, fundamentally an act of sabotage, an overload, "sabotage and withdraw."[41] Blocking circulations is a key preliminary to weakening circuits and burning them down and out when they try to reassert themselves. "Capital circulates or it dies."[42] For a communization that boils over the coils of cybernetic governance, allowing for new forms of community, new movements of solidarity, and new points of rest and care, we must blockade, accelerate, intensify, and burn our way out. We must therefore understand the governing machineries of our time.

ADDENDUM. SIGNAL AND NOISE: THE MAP VS THE TERRITORY

The desire to manage unpredictability with informational technology is not inherently that of a technocrat or a control freak. Information technology has great potential. Take a sensor that records blood-sugar levels, solving the problem of information as to when a (type one) diabetic would need to inject insulin or consume sugars. The problem occurs when an informational mapping of all of the signals that are useful for management and regulation gets confused with the territory. The map only provides signals of what it maps. A punitive relation to what is mapped is the problem — especially when it comes to information about body and mind. The territory is always manifesting noises that exceed the ability for the mapping to reduce everything to useful signals, which inform the practice of regulating said territory. Confusing the map for the territory results in a paranoid attempt to make signals out of noise or to silence the excess in the name of secure management — demanding that everything fit the program.

We say enthusiastically: The Territory is not indebted to its Map.

What cannot be informative to regulation, metastability, or security in a territory is something that always exceeds what is informative. It is noise. The problem of noise is a problem of managing what is left over from the clean-cut striations of the map: it is waste-management. Who decides what is noise and what signals the melodiousness of a new music? All creativity is noise to the old guard. Noise itself is often regulated, these days, through the proper controls. Regulated noise is given an informed rhythm in tightly controlled bursts, and this rhythm signals that even this excess has become sanitized. Yet, it is only noise which can boil over and terraform our land, to the panic of our cybernetic cartographers who wish to tame it into neat packets of enclosed information. Noise, of course, can have its own rhythm, and can be a signal unto itself and those encoded in its tones that can make it nourishing to an insurgent consciousness. It is, after all, only noise to the system which refuses to recognize it for the sake of its own continuity of government. What was noise to the slave master in Haiti was ultimately the signal which sounded out as the rallying cry, the signaling of "the very screams that open the way into the knowledge of slavery and the knowledge of freedom."[43]

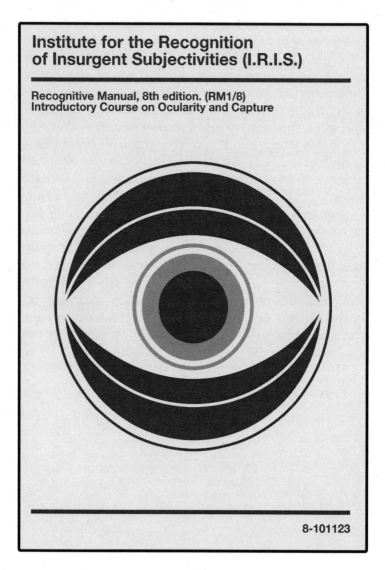

Institute for the Recognition of Insurgent Subjectivities (I.R.I.S.)

Recognitive Manual, 8th edition. (RM1/8)
Introductory Course on Ocularity and Capture

8-101123

Institute for the Recognition of Insurgent Subjectivities (I.R.I.S.) Recognitive Manual, 8th edition. RM1/8

COUNTER-INSURGENCY OF THE EYE: A MANUAL FOR THE PRACTICE OF OCULARITY

How are identities produced and maintained under conditions of domination and control? How does capital organize you so that it can recognize you? How is identity regulated in terms of who you can be and what you can become? What technologies police identity, and what are they afraid of? If you were to write a manual, a catalog, a primer, on how control societies manage, police, and establish forms of controlled identity, what would it look like?

INTRODUCTION: WHAT IS "OCULARITY"?

The term "ocularity" refers to the practice, or set of practices, which materially construct, produce, and police the limits of embodied identity and the potentialities of social and individual becoming. The purpose of this introductory manual is to provide an overview of some of the main techniques of ocular practice. Here at I.R.I.S., we pride ourselves on presenting the finest selections of ocular devices and apparatuses. Whilst we can't take credit for their invention, our purpose is to research, collect, and catalog the means and modes of identity-production and regulation as part of our work as a consulting service for cybernetic governance in the twenty-first century. We're the McKinsey of controlled subjectivity, the Deloitte of societal taxonomy, and we're here to help.

So what does it mean to practice "ocularity"? Ocularity is a practice of capture; ocularity captures via identification and the regulation of identities — what one can be, and what one cannot be in the eyes of recognition and recognizing power. Ocularity controls the identities of embodied political subjects by enclosing them within an ocular space, a controlled territory. Ocular space is maintained by a practice of force that sustains its boundaries, divisions, and contours; as an enclosure of those within ocularity. An ocular space is a space of closed possibilities of identification. Within such a space, the embodiment and practice of selfhood is delimited in advance (feedforward), and perturbations in the system of classifications are contained and redirected to the best of the system's stability and self-reproduction (negative feedback).

To be within the space of ocularity is to be sensed by it — that is, to be impressed upon by the structuring classifications embedded in ocular practice, and to be recognized through those imprinted, ocular categories. Ocular practice is structural inscription at the same time as it is the recuperation and neutralization of deviancy from the identity-categories of social experience. The categories or classes of ocularity are its active processes of categorizing and policing subjects according to such classifications; they are forms of social recognition that police the body, thought, and imagination. Functions and practices of recognition inscribe meanings that allow for the identification of subjects, not only through the shaping of their bodies, but the shaping of their self-conscious identifications and in how others consciously and unconsciously identify them.

When ocularity is operating in a productive way, it functions in a manner that proliferates and reinforces those forms. Actively learning and self-reinforcing recognitive practices of ocularity attempt to prevent, expose, or to delimit in advance; they are attempts at social, political, or cultural disruption. This delimiting consists in setting limits to the agents of disruption by identifying them, so as to pre-empt them or to defuse insurgent potential from achieving system-meltdown.

The disruption which ocular practice historically attempts to avert is insurgency, and the space in which an insurgency can brew is a space of non-ocularity or counter-ocularity; of escape from social forms of identification that have not (yet, at least) been recuperated by the forces that can enclose and identify them. This non-ocular space we call the "conspiratorial." The conspiratorial is the womb of insurgency as the *unidentified* (or poorly/fleetingly identified) threat to the security of social control. The problem of the insurgent is a problem of information.

From received intelligence, the theorists of the insurgent know this themselves, insofar as "minoritarian" guidelines to conducting civil war "dictate that one should enter the field anonymously as a purely abstract figure, because to appear as a subject whose identity is known marks one for death before the battle has even begun."[1] Contemporary cyber-capitalist governance sees security and control primarily as a problem of information in pre-empting disturbances, and so the un-identified has been centered as a problem of information (for security's sake). Hence, the "same basic algorithm computers use for sorting images also guides missile navigation systems, criminal-gait-analysis profiling, and all facial recognition software. Figures of anonymity exploit the vulnerabilities created in these systems."[2] There are exceptions in war, of course, but ocularity surrenders its relevance where the abstract violence of total annihilation begins (e.g., carpet bombing, nuclear holocaust).

The "eye" of ocularity is not a merely receptive eye; it does not simply receive objects as they are. Instead, the eye of ocularity perceives them according to pre-established standards of objectivity. The eye therefore corrects that which deviates from such standards in objective forms of mediation. The eye mediates what it sees in order to render it recognizable, i.e., so that it conforms to the categories of recognition and identification under which it is shaped into an object "proper" to the standards of "valid" objectivity. The eye of ocularity sees us, and in seeing it projects force onto what it sees; it remakes the object — to the best of its ability — in its own image. Like a Kantian awareness that encounters an affectation of its sense organs by an unknown external thing, it captures it by molding it in a form pre-determined by the activity of its sensing it. Ocularity constitutes what it captures at the same time that it captures it.[3] Ocularity preserves itself through a monopoly on identity and socially-recognized meaning over the spaces in which it is practiced. In placing that which is sensed under the conditions of its objectivity, it does great violence upon its object in sensing it. It is a net of libidinally enforced social axioms about the limits of identity. What this means is that ocular practice aims to limit the social consequences of *what* a body can do, what a body can *be recognized as being able to do,* and as such, what one *can desire to be or become.* (For ocularity, there is no difference, but all hope is dangerous).

Oculus is at work everywhere.

The space of ocularity has as its structural principle the eye of organizing and organized power, but much like the eye as it occurs in nature, the creator was not quite ontologically parsimonious enough with its quantitative distribution. Insurrection claims that it must defeat the eye in "becoming imperceptible." To this extent, I.R.I.S. exists to combat insurgency, and in particular insurgent identities, and the development of ocular practice and its theorization is what is at stake in this introductory manual. We hope that our think-tank will provide apt consultation to your governmental or extra-governmental agency, for all your recognitive counter-insurgent needs!

Remember: it is ocularity and security versus anonymity, counter-ocularity, and insurgency. As ocular scientists François Guéry and Didier Deleule have definitively established:

Identity is, in effect, a relation to anonymity. Only the unknown, the undifferentiated, the anonymous have need of a name and number. That anyone at all, whoever it may be, may be unknown and therefore threatening is the reality, the universe, of the one who guards property.[4]

Ocularity safeguards the propriety of identities and

the security of the realm of the self as it can and ought to be thought and lived. Against the conspiratorial, against the insurrection.

1.0. THE FUNDAMENTAL PRECONDITION OF ANY CONSPIRATORIAL ANALYSIS

The essence of the conspiracy is that its presence is always already withdrawing from the eyes of the investigator. The conspiracy withdraws from sight, and yet its withdrawal is a continuous process rather than an event. A good conspiracy understands the nature of the ocular, what it means to be seen, in order to trace those lines that run counter to the directions of visibility, be they lines occluded from the ocular scope, or that these lines can be bent and refracted over and around the body of the conspirator(s). At most, the presence of a conspiracy is something presupposed by the investigating agency. Yet, in a successful process of conspiracy, this presence is not captured by its seeking. The investigative eye, fundamentally opposed to the conspiracy, is always in a process of capturing that the conspiratorial aims to constantly withdraw from. The conspiratorial is that which is always attempting its withdrawal from ocular reception, as well as ocular comprehension; becoming incomprehensible — out of sight and out of mind. Nonetheless, when conspiratorial or insurgent forces make an escape from the confines of ocular space, they leave traces of withdrawal and fugitive residue. This is why a true conspiracy invites the terror of an ocular paranoia, through its own spectral capture of the eye that seeks to capture *it*. The conspiratorial lives rent-free in the eye of power, even by its most ghostly image.

An expedient conspiracy is one that births *insurgencies* by provoking martial-political overreactions — the *iron fists* of the paranoiac state — that themselves often provoke the eruption of insurgent force and a corresponding popular support.[5] From the standpoint of counter-insurgency studies, this is not necessarily a bad tactic, given the "iron fist" method has proven to be notoriously hit-and-miss.[6] As such, it is paramount for the security of any nation that faces the threat of insurgency that it understands its *own* ocularity: the ability to not merely see conspiratorial forces, but to *recognize* them; to place them under clearly defined and substantial schemas or identities through this recognition. The intent is to *capture* these forces within a counter-display of force, such that this dispels them of their conspiratorial — and hence proto-insurgent — character. In doing so, we may begin to understand our current mechanisms of ocularity and ocular capture, and can therefore grasp the counter-conspiratorial — and hence counter-insurgent — limits of ocularity.

The aim of this manual is to clarify the field of ocular science. This will aid practitioners in designing systems of security both in terms of stability and when it comes to understanding our schemas of recognizing, identifying, capturing, and finally *dissolving* proto-insurgent conspiratorial units. The need for this manual has only grown in light of recent insurrections, and the theorists of insurgency know it. Take, for example, the George Floyd rebellion and the resultant attempt at counter-insurgency. As Idris Robinson summarizes:

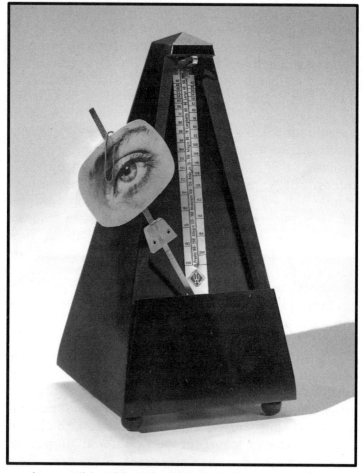

Indestructible Object (or Object to Be Destroyed), Man Ray (Emmanuel Radnitzky) (American, 1890–1976)

While spearheaded by a Black avant-garde, this largely multi-ethnic rebellion managed to spontaneously overcome codified racial divisions. The containment of the revolt aims at reinstating these rigid lines of separation and policing their boundaries.[7]

As such, this text will attempt to lay out a brief outline of the practice and possibilities of ocularity as a concept of counter-conspiratorial counter-insurgency.

2.0. THE MECHANISMS OF OCULARITY

2.1. OCULARITY AS GENERAL ACTIVITY: "SENSING," OCULAR VS CONSPIRATORIAL SPACE, AND CATEGORIZATION

Contemporary counter-insurgent thought takes as its theoretical basis a wide variety of conceptual tools for its analysis of ocularity as a social and political phenomenon. We understand that the essential function of mechanisms that practice and produce ocularity is to capture the sense or meaning of an individual or group of individuals, and to recognize them by placing them under a certain identity category. This is not simply a passive practice of recording the identities that are seen and "capturing" them within tables of data, demographic distributions, or within the judicial bounds of legal or illegal identities. Rather, ocularity is a practical and active social process of inscriptive force. The sense of such an identity can be something that is conformed to via social disciplinary mechanisms, such as medical prescription, martial training, or education. However, such ocular conformity can also be engendered by more subtle restrictions on the actions of those so-identified, such as restrictions applied to social and private space, i.e., educational spaces, cultural spaces, forms of employment, territorial-political boundaries, and within a systematically limited transport infrastructure.

The *sense* of an identity is something that is constituted and impressed upon the bodies of those identified as such. Identification is a process of impressing the ocularity-prescribed social meaning onto the body of the recipient through the "forces" of the ocular,[8] by which they are seen. Force imposes and holds onto the social meaning of a body when it becomes a subject enclosed in ocular space. Ocular apparatuses record people's bodies under certain schemata at the same time that it writes these identifications upon them. Ocularity — by which we mean, *good* ocular practice — leaves nothing hidden to conspiracy; it aims to identify every enemy and occlude the possibility of the enemy escaping into an unidentified and unregulated novel form.

Ocularity must not be understood as a nomadic force external to the mechanisms of state and society. As a counter-insurgency mechanism, it cannot be seen as a machine of war upon something outside of the state.[9] Ocularity does not "smooth out" the space of the conspiracy. The conspiratorial space is always smooth, undifferentiated, at once everywhere and nowhere in space, counting down the days until its plan comes to fruition. Ocularity "striates" space, regiments it, establishes clear lines and gradients of identity, practices of recognitive conformity, and exclusivity. If there is any ocular war, it is civil war and its management, or as a response to unconventional warfare in counter-insurgent practice. This was the conclusion of the authors of the *Tiqqun* journal, who uncovered as part of their "civil war theory" of proto-insurgent conspiratorialism that "To be recognized is to be seized and positioned in relation to over social bodies and for this positioning to be striated and asserted as a *finality*."[10]

Ocular recognition delimits the possibilities of identity in advance and applies a constant stream of force to maintain the senses of these identity-recognitive categories. This force must be maintained in order to consistently occlude the possibility of a smooth, conspiratorial space.

What can be concluded from this is that ocular recognition is not simply an immediate cognitive act of receiving that which is seen by the ocular mechanisms. Rather, as the theorist and recognitive-machinist G.W.F. Hegel has noted, sensing a body is never immediate nor purely receptive; it is always involved in the active process of mediating the data received under universal linguistic categories.[11] The recognition enacted by ocularity is an expression of the forces and apparatuses of that state society whose ocularity is being deployed. The recognition, or sensing of individuals and groups by ocularity, is the mediation of these individuals and groups such that each is forced into the categories that make up the legal, customary, and institutional language of that society and the practice of reproducing said society. Ocularity is interwoven into the fabric of a society's actual culture and institutional systems and subsystems of organization.[12]

Ocularity should therefore aim to be the practice of generating an "ocular culture" that can preserve, manage, and proliferate patterns of recognition and identification that "always keep the lights on" to avoid the conspiratorial. This culture maintains a language of identity and categorization that is constantly striating the space of society by impressing onto individuals and groups an identity that is promoted by societal and cultural institutions as substantial and authoritative. These ocular impressions must be taken by those within this culture with minimal agony, with minimized antagonism (or at least, a controlled and defused antagonism, a thermostatic social heat). An ocular culture is an essential component in the social production of subjectivities. The subject is hence, as philosopher Shelley Tremain clarifies: "an effect of force relations continuously constituted and reconstituted through concrete and institutional practices and discourses over the course of its life-time."[13]

In his phenomenological experiments regarding simulated ocularity, Hegel himself noted that the collapse of Robespierre's regime during the French Revolution was tied to the very absence of ocularity that was inherent to the regime's schema of its subjects. Under this regime, the language of identification was entirely vague, purely universal, abstractly negative, and yet actively anti-conspiratorial. The subject brought under ocularity was entirely absent in any concrete manner, apart from the undefined category of "the People" or "the citizen" and their entirely vague and un-identifiable "General Will" adapted from Rousseau's democratic theory. Hegel notes that this level of ocularity was itself suicidal in its incompetence, and as such could not identify or comprehend its own ocular deficiencies as its greatest threat, leading Robespierre to be executed under the auspices of his own ocular dissolution mechanism — the guillotine.

This mechanism of the guillotine became a tool of the conspiratorial forces of the Thermidorian insurgency: a corrective force wielded by fellow "citizens" as avatars of the same, vague banner of "the People" in whose revolutionary name so many heads were removed.[14] The conspirators had no identity recognizable by the security services. They remained in the shadows of the eye that could only see the blur of an abstract "traitor" who could be anyone. The ocular state of the Reign of Terror could therefore do nothing but stab wildly into the masses until its terror had created the regime's own executioners.

A vague ocularity widens the scope of those who fall under the cloak of the conspiratorial. If the categories of your ocularity lack sufficient regimentation, striation, or recognitive practice, then every person can — and eventually will — conspire against you.

NOTE: This is a partial benefit of welfare states. For example, in their destruction of highly anonymized urban slums in favor of highly regimented and registered social housing programs, they eliminate the anonymity offered to many conspiratorials who fall outside the zones of intense ocular surveillance.[15] Tenants are identified, catered for, and some of the material privations that would inspire insurgencies are defused. In the winding down of many of these states, it should be noted that whilst the material support offered is becoming less and less, the recording mechanisms (social security numbers, medical records, birth certificates, employment histories, as well as non-welfarist mechanisms such as credit scores) will still remain in full employment. For example, I.R.I.S.'s primary recommendations to the British government have been that the National Health Service (NHS) should be preserved as a centralized biopolitical mechanism of recording and population management. The NHS has a near-sacred status to the populace, and in recording all identities and modes of the body and of the self, it equally holds the power to set medical limits, as well as enforce and reinforce moral and judicial ones both institutionally and in setting the wider "common sense" of the population, who look to it as a beacon of national morality and near-omnibenevolent care. Even if all such care is to be provided by private enterprise in the future, the centrality and political efficacy of the recording mechanism that distributes such provisions, in light of its popular moral legitimacy, should not be sacrificed if there is to be a high-ocularity practice on that island.

Medical ocularity will be further examined in the later sections of this manual.

2.2. OCULARITY AND DIFFERENCE

The conclusion that the field of ocular counter-insurgency has drawn from these cases of successful conspiratorialism — of which the Thermidor is taken to be an exceptionally salient paradigm case — is that the intensity of recognitive capture-power within in an ocular space is directly proportional to the multiplicity of ocular categories within said space. Put simply, the more cells in said space, the greater the number of potential insurgents can be situated within it before they can follow their paths of escape into the smooth space of the conspiratorial. Robespierre's low-intensity ocular practice recognized only two categories as exhibited in the practices of his government: "the People" and "the counter-revolutionary," and famously the vagueness and indeterminacy of these categories made identification an arbitrary and capricious practice, through which concrete threats were left undetermined, and hence conspiratorial.

In contrast, a high-intensity practice of the ocular would embody in its cultural, legal, and political practice a well-defined set of recognitive categories. These categories aid the identification of potential insurgents and hence occlude their escape into the conspiratorial by re-situating their sense of themselves and how society sees them — and each seeing is actualized in their social activity — within the ocular field of vision, the striated spatial field of state power. A higher plurality of ocular categories is a lower flow of smoothness within and across the ocular space. Categories can be generated or stabilized as intersections between multiple ocular categories. In such a case, ocularity enforces the intersection between multiple of its own categories as itself a distinct, policed category.

This is not to say that contemporary developments in social justice movements from the late-twentieth century onwards have been beneficial to ocularity. Indeed, the production of new identities outside of ocular production harbor their own danger that researchers of our own as well as those of similar organizations have attempted to address. The aim of ocular practice is not the maintenance of any particular identity *as such*, but is fundamentally a management strategy for identity and identification in general. Its aim is ultimately control, and where fluidity of identity is present, a regulated plasticity of selfhood is necessary. Ocularity names this the Abstract Machine that polices the limits of identification, both for those within the bounds of "normality" and for those designated as outside of it.

3.0. PLASTICITY, OCULARITY, AND SPECULATIVE NEUROLOGY: THE SCIENCE OF PRODUCING RECOGNITIVE-CONFORMING AFFECTS IN SOCIAL REASONING

In our current era of technological and political acceleration — one exacerbated by plague, economic collapse, and geopolitical insecurity — the counter-insurgent science of ocularity has had to make its own leaps into new fields of scientific knowledge. The ultimate goal of ocular practice is not only to see into people's heads, but to organize their heads into that which ocularity recognizes, into a neurological instance of ocular categories. Contemporary Spinozist turns in neurology have recently begun to make this possible. The revelatory promise of neuro-plasticity and its Spinozist deployments have now opened up new ocular possibilities. These new frontiers of practice allow us to speculate on how recognitive forms can be cognitively and *physically* implanted.

I.R.I.S. has explored this potential most notably through the work of the philosophical neuro-technician Catherine Malabou. Malabou invokes Demasio's Spinozist neurology to explain the indifferent coldness that occurs when a person's identity is severely traumatized or destroyed, leaving them indifferent to the emotional or affective concerns when tackling social decisions around conflict and risk. Such social decisions regarding the risks to be taken, and the decision to engage in social conflict, are themselves crucial in any question of conspiratorial allegiance and practice. The hypothesis deployed in Malabou's analysis is Demasio's conception of the "somatic markers" in the brain that give certain kinds of emotional weight to certain options in decision-making.[16] This weight-distribution is governed by the Spinozian axis of "joys" and "sorrows," where the former expresses an expansion of an individual's capacities and the latter expresses a dampening.[17] The capacities under such a regime of affective governance are that of high-level cognitive functions necessary for social life and decision-making: memory, language, attentiveness, and reasoning.[18] Whilst we lack the current medical capacities to engineer ocularly aligned somatic markers within the brain from birth or infancy, the dual function of the neuro-plastic is that which grounds our potential to ocularly re-mold and distribute these markers to fit ocular-compliant schemas — with these schemas being those of social language, self-identification, norms of rationality, and the affective pull that ocular culture has on the attention of individuals.

The goal of ocular culture is to occlude the capacities of the individual life. This is not only done post-birth, but also in anticipation of their birth. In high-intensity ocular practices, the individual life is detected, or sensed, even before it is sensed empirically. This is because what is sensed as socially legitimate under ocularity is simply what is sensible, i.e., what is permissible to its sensibility and the forms of judgment that structure it into a coherent identity.[19] When it comes to the plastic element of the brain and the affective dimension of the living individual, I.R.I.S.'s eventual goal is to shepherd the distribution of somatic markers towards an affective weight into ocularity-compliant distributions.

Above all, the attentiveness to one's own plasticity must be avoided if ocularity is to be maintained. In extreme circumstances, the potential for "destructive" plasticity must be deployed, in the sense that the individual must be made indifferent to their possibility of being other than within an ocular schema — a totally negative deployment of a traumatic severing of those affective distributions that exceed the ocular schemata. There must be no outside of ocularity — that is, the smooth space of the conspiratorial. The ocular subject must be prevented from distributing emotional weight towards any non-ocular affectivity at all costs. They must not even "*lack*" when it comes to their sense of themselves in ocularity,[20] but must be wholly indifferent to the outside, to any escape from ocular space. What they are for the ocular should be what they are for themselves, with the right of change being dictated in advance by the former. The limits of the ocular should be the limits of the narrative of any life within the ocular field in which this life finds itself.

Overall, we can conclude that, in an optimal situation, their indifference would be conditioned into them as a total absence of *imagination* when it comes to the outside. We understand that, under certain clinical rubrics, these ocularity tactics may be recognized as the induction of trauma, and as such bear the possibility of counter-ocular healing (especially in such a highly speculative and experimental field that we and other counter-insurgency operators are working in). However, others in our field have made great strides in acting to prevent this psychological rejuvenation. The most notable of all these is the method of re-imposing ocularity when it comes to the identity of the psychologically alienated. Famously,

Deleuze and Guattari identified and refined this method in its Freudian and Kleinian formulations in their theory of "oedipalization," in which all attempts at understanding psychological trauma become confined in the familial triangle of Freud's Oedipal complex, in which everything is tied to one's relation within the triangular identity of daddy-mommy-me, from the private to the public, from the personal to the political, and ever more.[21] The ocularity of oedipalization, if we are to draw upon the myth, is to prevent *oedipism*, or the removal of one's eyes. Deleuze and Guattari hence leave us with a term for an anti-ocular practice that we shall develop further through an examination of recent trends in conspiratorialism.

If we are to take further examples of ocular practices in current use, the phenomenon of "Capitalist Realism," identified by the hyperstitional entity known as "k-punk," shows itself as an imperfect ocularity, which ocular science aims to improve on. Nonetheless, the CR-division of ocular science over in the UK has made substantial strides in developing "post-historical" methods of shifting affective weight away from the notion of the outside in the form of an "alternative" to capitalist economic systems. This has been achieved through a collaboration of journalistic, educational, and entertainment-media apparatuses. Each has done their part in the generation of an affect of "reflexive impotence," by which individuals identify across a multiplicity of identity categories. Regardless of the number of categories, they are all delimited within the recognition that alternative social relations — and hence, social ways of life that would constitute identities outside of ocular culture and space — are *a priori* impossible.[22] However, the reflexivity of this impotence itself has generated a self-consciousness of this lack, and as such has created a desire-formulation that, whilst seemingly a "lack," is actually a productive line, one that looks for an exit, and hence a line of flight with conspiratorial potential. The line of flight enacted by the k-punk phenomenon still haunts us.

We nonetheless remain confident in our abilities to effectively block the flows of conspiratorial desire when it comes to the contemporary information era — the self-conscious capitalist realists have only ever romanticized about an image of the possibility of an outside; they as yet lack the imagination to believe it can be possibly reached, and remain as effectively and affectively hopeless as before.

The intersection of ocularity, psychology, and neurology is the awakening and management of the dormant forces of plasticity. We aim to control both the creative plasticity that forms the affective markers that determine social cognition, and the destructive plasticity required to accelerate the neurological deterioration of those affective capacities that resist ocular capture by imagining otherwise — that resist *oculus*.

Ocularity draws its self-differentiation from its own plasticity, where an eye can become the hand that writes on the bureaucrat's form, the tongue that proclaims with signifying authority the identity of its target, the ear that may expose the conspiratorial by wiretapping insurgent lines of escape. The ocular eye is indeed an organ, but it also is an implant. It is a functional, abstract, organizing code diffused across the bodies enclosed and regulated within ocular space. If conspiratorialism were to truly become eyeless, they would hardly be able to see if they had any organs at all.

4.0. OCULAR INTERVENTION UPON THE BODY AND ITS ORGANS

An identity as a recognized self-consciousness always has empirical, embodied, and affective aspects. What is implicit or unconscious in the identification within an ocular space of sensing bears itself to expression in action. In being submitted to the recognition of others, what is recognized is almost always, inescapably, the presentation of a body. One even presents a body in cyberspace, through avatars and gestures of communication that direct the receiver to forming a certain image of the sender. The recognition of a body that corresponds to an identity is not a recognition of its properties of spatial extension as such (the number of certain parts and their sizes, mounds, folds, protrusions, and extremities of the flesh), but what meanings, codes, or significations are attached to certain aspects of a body and the expressive use of it. Ocularity codes aspects of a body, writes its categories upon its parts, and even divides the smooth surface of a flesh into such regions that can be called "parts" that place one within a set of ocular categories. (As we shall see, a paradigmatic case of bodily ocularity is that of the sensing of sexuation in the ocularization of genitalia). Ocularity maps the body and surveys its regions, drawing borders and declaring sovereign jurisdictions upon its territory. This mapping occurs with a baptismal violence that often ignores the yearnings and differences that are suffocated under the cartographer's parchment and the blade of his pen. It is baptismal because it inaugurates the community as defined by ocular categories, as bound to its new borders, by which it becomes recognized as the sovereign house of social activity.

Bodily ocularity is an ocular technique that determines the field of admissible identities in relation to norms of "acceptable" bodily characteristics and expressions. As a negative feedback mechanism, it responds to perturbations in the controlled standards of the flesh. It reshapes bodies into its preconceived schema of valid and controlled identifications. This can be exposited through some of the most common examples of bodily ocularity and the interventions upon the body that ocular practice may entail. The following examples are given to provide the ocular practitioner with a sense of the craft by which bodies are molded by both creative and destructive means, towards certain systematically programmed recognition patterns.

Ocularity, in determining recognizable identities, naturally brings itself to the social scene as a practice of establishing, maintaining, and regulating what it identifies in advance as "normality." Ocularity normalizes. Luckily, most will already fit into the ocular categories of normality (especially if the field of ocular practice is already stable). If not, certain regulatory inventions, and bodily *interventions*, are often needed. These interventions are both symbolic as well as physical, and are indeed often indifferent to the distinction. For the writing-in of a meaning onto the body is achieved by the incision of the re-coding, re-organizing apparatus. It is the bladed pen of the cartographer, the invasion of the surface by a pointed and directed intent to signify upon that body. Ocularity is the colonizer of the body; it marks space in order to mark its territory, in order to occupy it. Ocularity designates the body *terra nullius*, as if it has the sole claim over a territory. Ocular inscription must also therefore contain a capacity for erasure, in erasing the competing codes, meanings, and cultural heritages of the body upon which ocularity intervenes. As will be shown further on in this manual, this capacity for erasure generates its own problematics for ocular practice.

4.1. OCULAR TECHNIQUES AND INTERVENTIONS

4.1.1. SEX AND GENDER AS POLICED AND POLICING CATEGORIES

Simply put, many cases of ocular intervention upon and *into* the body are either disciplinary, cosmetic, or both. An ocular intervention can often be painful and lifelong, insofar as it marks upon the body a certain shape or code by which it is to be recognized as belonging to such-and-such a category. The code or shape — or more precisely, the *normalized category* — produced on the body is itself the point of such an intervention, and high-ocularity societies make common use of them. As a first example, there is the case of the intersex body and its treatment within a society where concepts of binary sex (dimorphism) serve as the justificatory ground of limiting identities within certain gender categories by mandating biological conformity to the more expressive, cultural categories of gender.[23] In such societies, ambiguity of categorization is a risk that many refuse to accommodate, and intervention must be made so as to determine the *truth* of an individual's biological sex, according to certain standards of knowledge.[24]

Ocular practice within some regions, such those

of continental Europe, was previously quite low-intensity regarding the body of the intersex person. For example, in the case of bodily (and, of course, genital) ambiguity, the right of assigning the "true" sex of the intersexed body was determined by the paternal figure of the father or godfather.[25] Now, however, ocular practice has turned more to a model based on medical and scientific forms of knowledge as a sanction for the fixing of categories. This model relies upon the use of institutions that produce and reinforce figures of those "supposed to know." These practices of institutional knowledge primarily specialize in normalization (healthy vs. sick, disorderly vs. orderly), and from an apparent position of objectivity that is commonly taken as near-absolute.

Under this practice — which ocular practitioners may have to re-evaluate in light of the insurgent movement for intersex rights — where sexual binaries are held as ocularly beneficial to maintain, the intersex body is identified but not allowed to remain as a properly valid identity. Medically, doctors invade the intersex body to find the "true" identifying organs underneath, to examine which organs are more prominent so as to bring them into accordance with sex-norms, and to even possibly remove what is seen as an ambiguity-provoking excess of biological organization and tissue.[26] Doctors, as biological technicians and regulators of what is known as "normal functioning," legislate the identity and the shape of the body. They legislate and practice their techniques of biological and categorical sculpture according to ocular schemas, i.e., the rules of the game of a medical craft shaped by ocular categories. Indeterminacy is insecurity. Any ambiguity in the categorization of a subject often translates into ambiguities regarding their context and rights as a legal person, particularly when it comes to gendered property laws generated from institutions of marriage, etc.

Certain bodies that do not fit within the ocular schemas of law exist only as affronts to the law's universal application, because they are given to the law and yet simultaneously exceed the rules of the game: the names, functions, and rules that govern each piece in its place and conduct. They embarrass its universality as the real living incompleteness of the law, which legislates over the intercourse of the lives under its jurisdiction and assessment. Bodily ocularity is hence a key matter for law and order, against anarchy, against "monstrous" embarrassments.[27] They are "monstrous" in the manner of an ocular monster, as one "whose face, body, and behaviors cannot yet be considered true in a predetermined regime of knowledge and power" in the ocular sense.[28] This legislation that unites the medical and juridical (as a valid life for legislation over in the manner of *personhood*) often if not always happens from birth, so as to prevent the formation of an intersex character as a lifelong endeavor. Such a program of ocular post-natal or even *pre*-natal screening has already been proposed in one of the most concrete texts in the canon of ocularity, Kathryn Pauly Morgan's articulation of the "Gender DiMorph Utopia,"[29] in which Morgan advises ocular practitioners that

> ambiguous babies (i.e., babies with ambiguous genitalia) are to be labelled "temporarily intersexed" and surgically corrected as soon after birth as possible so that they may fit into their proper gender location. All requests for gender-related research in fetal endocrinology, fetal surgery, and

plastic genital surgery should receive full funding. Innovations in these vital areas of research should receive the wide public recognition and esteemed awards that they deserve.[30]

Whilst we, as in section 3.0, wholly recognize the plasticity of the biological — how else could we shape it? — ocularity resolves itself to confine this plasticity within its categories for their stability. The categories may themselves evolve as could the practice of their enforcement, but this is by no means viable for most ocular societies and ocular cultures. Ocular interventions upon the intersex body stratify — if not neutralize — bodily difference for the sake of recognition. The plasticity of the biological can and *does* serve the ocular, as exemplified in the case of the intersex person. The surgical intervention upon their body does not "fix" their organs in themselves, but fixes them *to* an ocular category. The category that they are fixed *to* is gender as distributed across X number of categories, but almost always binary. That the plasticity of the flesh can be made to conform to the categories of gender — which are presented as fixed and immutable — is the end goal of the ocular intervention. The simple categorization of gender secures the sexual from the insecurity of its anarchy, its "incoherence" and non-conformism.[31] This operation is part of the technique that secures gender as a mechanism in an ocular culture.

Insofar as this practice is often utilized to sustain binary categories of recognition such as those of sex — which is not biological, but a categorization of forms of biology into recognized "types" across a binary system — this is equally done for the enforcement of the categories of gender that reinforce the sexual categories (which *are* what we assign as "the sexual") in turn. This itself generates a biopsychosocial feedback loop of recognitive ocularity. We have made considerable innovations even in light of the return of post- or non-binaric gender categories. These categories were previously suppressed under state-colonial and colonial-Catholic ocularities — particularly in indigenous cultures — from their recognition and expression.[32] One technique developed by ocular technicians at I.R.I.S. is the re-imposition of biological views of binary sexual Dimorphism via the "AMAB-AFAB" binary — Assigned Male at Birth, Assigned Female at Birth) — applied retrospectively to transgender individuals (binary as well as non-binary) in order to tie them back to the medical sense of authority through which Dimorphic ocularity operates. Where this practice is not in operation, ocular forces instead rely on the solidification of the non-binary gender as a simple "synthesis" or middle-term that ought to be recognized as a simple third, composite gender of the poles of Male and Female. This is the ocular practice of CompAnd, or "Compulsory Androgyny," designed to maintain non-binary bodies within a recognized set of gendered tropes, subverting their attempt at a deconstruction of the very history and force of the binary system in which non-binary individuals find themselves. The "truth" of the gender of their bodies and how they are presented is hence fixed at a maintained and secured point of ambiguity, although this latter innovation is one with a predominantly cultural emphasis. In every case outline, ocularity senses by sexing, and it sexes with a gendered and gendering eye.

However, regarding gendered and gendering ocularity, the in-demand techniques of the twenty-first century are far less taxonomically subtle. Recent developments in anglosphere and European client nations have shown an accelerating political will towards ocular restriction and the identification of certain categories for elimination entirely from the register of legitimate social existence. Various governmental bodies in the United States of America, for example, and a growing number of them, are identifying the transgendered body and subject as a conspiratorial identity against the familial, moral, and religious order of things. As a category of being and as a mode of becoming, it is now being openly proclaimed that anything beyond binaric gender and sexual dimorphism is fundamentally illegitimate, a social contagion, a hostile and conspiratorial category, a war-machine against the order of things.

With ontological terror, the current regimes respond with increasing degrees of ocular terrorism. The ocular techniques of identification for destruction are well-established, for they have been used before in the early stages of an isomorphic operation under the National Socialist regime in Germany: the elimination of the trans body from any access to healthcare, as was accelerated in their imprisonment and in the destruction of Hirschfeld's Institute for Sexual Science, where the earliest forms of trans healthcare were pioneered in a place of refuge; the demonization of the existence and unfolding of trans expression as a conspiracy linked to the ocular category of "Judeo-Bolshevism" (or "Cultural Marxism" in its modern guise); and the press's own generation of stochastic terrorist discourses, which place the existence of the ocularized subject under "question" and *as* a question — one which, by implication, can never be answered (for fear of silencing the sanctity of "debate" with which the press identity themselves) except in the circumstances that the category of person under question is reduced to a state of non-existence.

These techniques are well-established, but risky. They resemble the "iron first" approach to social confrontation we established earlier, and risk provoking a solidarity amongst the wider populace that could put the ocular practitioners into peril. This is exacerbated by the historical fact that such techniques often spiral into other social domains where a governmental regime feels threatened. Exterminationism never exhausts itself on its first targets. Nonetheless, the historical examples of exterminationism provide what we can only call the first ocular register or catalog that so clearly illustrates its structure and purpose. See below.

What is important as an illustration here is not the colors or badges, but the grid, the matrix of identification, and the material forces that reinforce them and execute their function. I.R.I.S. prides itself on its historical accuracy and faithfulness to the practices of the moment, and so we have taken care to provide only the most accurate, isomorphic examples. I.R.I.S. does not, however, specify in such blunt approaches to ocularity, but they nonetheless extend to the interventions upon the body we analyze in their history and continued use. Presently, exterminationist techniques are ascendant but only in parallel with practices of medicalization and pathologization that solidify the identification of groups with illness to be removed or remedied (for example, the medicalization of transness within the *DSM-III* [*Diagnostic and Statistical Manual*], which is itself an exemplary ocular schema). The intersections

MARKINGS OF CAMP INMATES IN THE CONCENTRATION CAMPS

Form and Color of Markings

	POLITICAL	HABITUAL CRIMINALS	EMIGRANTS	JEHOVAH'S WITNESSES	HOMO-SEXUALS	VAGRANTS
Basic Colors						
Markings for Repeaters						
Inmates of Penal Battalions						
Markings for Jews						
Special Markings	Race Defiler Male	Race Defiler Female	Escape Suspect	Number of Inmate (2307)	NUMBER OF INMATE — REPEATER — JEW-POLITICAL — MEMBER OF PENAL BATTALION — ESCAPE SUSPECT	
	P — Pole	T — Czech	Members of Armed Forces	Special Inmate		

Markings of Camp Inmates in the Nazi Concentration Camps. Each marker is placed within a cell within a matrix of identification for the sake of confining and ultimately eliminating those identified by them. This translated grid was sourced from the charity Liberate https://liberate.gg/lgbtq-history/nazi-camp-uniform-symbol/

of medical and gendering or sexuating ocularity begin our presentation of the following kinds of ocular interventions.

4.1.2. THE DISABLED BODY

Interventions for the sake of upholding and policing the bounds of the normal, the recognized, the categorizable, those interventions for the sake of what power desires to see in its subjects, are no less present in relation to the disabled body. The subsections of this portion of the manual do not refer to separate structures, nor even necessarily to different technologies, operations, or institutions, but only to emphasize different aspects of overlapping interventions of ocularity upon people's bodies. There is little structurally that can be said here that was not itself said in the discussion of the intersex body in terms of how disability is categorized and recognized in the ocular discourse. As the rights group Intersex Human Rights Australia note, the World Health Organization's definition of disability leads to the incorporation of the intersex category into this very definition — solidifying the intersex body as a medicalized one and candidate for intervention under current ocular regimes.[33]

People express identities through which they are recognized in multiple ways, through the meaning of the speech and writing as well as through bodily expression, or performing their active role in the social field, and the meanings that this body conveys and is recognized as conveying. As Judith Butler noted in a recent speech from 2012:

the performativity of the human animal takes place through gesture, gait, modes of mobility; through sound and image; through various expressive means that are not reducible to public forms of verbal speech.[34]

What one expresses is indeed a function of one's mobility, and mobility issues constitute one of the most common images of disability along with stance, orientation, and gait. Normalizing ocular power "corrects" or "fixes" the gait of a body so that it approximates the category, so that it "walks and stands normally." Even if this may be a painful process, this nonetheless situates such a body within the order of the normal, and may even be seen as a gift of normality in a society that recognizes the abnormal as monstrous, as discussed above. In the hospital, they are treated with the greatest hospitality, which is perilous to refuse, and in this they are *rehabilitated*, for the house of the ocular — in many such cases of ocular practice — is to be their home. Rehabilitation marks a profound advancement in ocular practice, for in Stiker's terms, it

marks the appearance of a culture that attempts to complete the act of identification, of making identical. This act will cause the disabled to disappear and with them all that is lacking, in order to assimilate them, drown them, dissolve them in the greater and single social whole.[35]

Rehabilitation is the integration of the body into its ocular home. From the standpoint of ocularity, it is as if the body failed to appear in a way ready-made for the home of society, and hence its homeliness is lacking in its abnormality. A home must be given again, as a replacement and re-integration of the abnormal body. The creation of so many disabled bodies from the wars of the early twentieth century and the accident-rich layout of industrial capitalism in the West led to a shift in the ocular language of disability towards rehabilitation, and to the removal of deficiencies in the body.[36] It is not simply that deficiencies are to be removed in the manner of "curing," as it relates simply to notions of health.[37] Health nonetheless plays a part, and whilst what warrants "sickness" intersects with ocular practice, doctors nonetheless exist for the provision of health as much as biological *regulation*. This latter element, the evaluating and resource-distributing function of the health provider/manager, functions by situating bodies within an ocular space in which their identity is no longer problematic, but legislated cleanly and smoothly regulated. As such:

Specificity and aberrancy are thereby forbidden and condemned. The different must be folded into the commonplace, into the accepted, into the recognized.[38]

In being provided ocular accommodation, it is not necessarily the case that the desires of the rehabilitated are accommodated for, and regularity is imposed beyond the "messiness" of desires, senses of dignity, and autonomy — for the regularity is recognized even in the absence of all of these. To repeat: What is aimed at is the production of regularity, stability — secure integration. Regularity is always the goal of regulation, for the ocular question is: "Who wouldn't want to be regular in the face of such a painful deficiency?" From there, rehabilitation enters the scene. Regularity is what is normal, what is recognizable, and in the context of disability can be shown explicitly in some ocular studies of rehabilitation in the case of paraplegics, such as those of Martin Sullivan, who summarizes the field thusly in cases of the regulation of bodily waste in those paralyzed in the lower body:

> Until a regime of regularity is imposed upon the evacuation of bodily wastes, the paraplegic body can hardly be considered docile. Thus, it is here, in the establishment of a regime of regularity, that the greatest struggle between medical power, the body, and the paraplegic subject takes place.
>
> Anatomy combined with technology means that males are confronted with far fewer problems than females in the area of bladder management. Some of the men in my research did, nonetheless, feel violated by the surgical procedure that had been performed on them to relieve ostensible problems with urine retention (which can have serious health consequences). These men, who were young at the time when the surgery was performed on them, now complain bitterly that they were not sufficiently counselled [sic] about the full implications of the procedure, which induces a continual, free flow of urine from the bladder. As one man remarked:

> > "I've had one of those; I was told I needed one. I wasn't really told what it was, what it would mean. The arrogance. Doctors, man. Arrogant bastards. . . . They gave me one. And they didn't have to."[39]

This may not seem "normal" in the constancy of urine flows, but it is regulated according to the norms of medical practice and the power invested in it. The body is docile, incorporated, controlled, and recognizable. Now that we know what is to be expected, rehabilitation can extend itself in terms of assimilation, which is always defined by the ocular categories of normality, manifesting in relation to the disabled as assimilation to the abled body and its evaluation in relation to this identified, normal standard. Especially under welfarist or self-cannibalizing welfarist states, the trend seems to be from internment of the disabled (both mentally and physically) towards a constant state of identification through evaluation. The *Oculus* of ocularity senses the body in the manner of evaluation. To paraphrase Kant, it is not a matter of making the ocular category adequate to the object it sees, but in making that object adequate to the ocular concept.[40] The disabled are put to the test of their adequation to the categorial ideal of the able body; the productive, recognizable, and hospitable body. Technologies of regulation, diagnosis, and sculpting of the plasticity of the biological advance, and so things are allowed to be more open, in spaces that are nonetheless in their openness tightly controlled.[41] Yet abnormality "is not allowed to go unchecked: physicians, judges, social workers provide control, proper functioning."[42]

These bodies in evaluation, as are all under ocular practice, are in debt[43] to their evaluator, to the social eye of recognizability for their social existence and the provision of care. As such, they can be compelled to account for the necessity of their continued presence accordingly, acquiescing to the ocular standard. This has been perfected in welfarist states such as the UK, with their constant assessments to conform to the ableist standard of "fit for work," invoked to deploy ocularity to compel more disabled people off of their financial supports and into the workforce in light of the financial crisis.[44]

This process by which ocularity both hyper-recognizes non-normality in the body, at the same time as it seeks to subject, regulate, or remove it from social presence and social production, is a psychological and corporeal molding of the body in ocular practice. The aim is to produce regulated people with regulated identifications of their own deficiencies, regulated at regular intervals through omnipresent evaluations of their aptness in an ocular space. Beyond the failures of Robespierre, as addressed in earlier sections with his vague and indeterminate categories by which those useful or damaging to society were evaluated, states with high-intensity ocular practice have successfully enacted a reign of hyper-specialized terror upon the disabled body. Sustaining such a wide net of technologies and diagnoses is imperative to the mass regulation of them in ocular practice, and Stiker summarizes the goals of I.R.I.S. regarding this matter clearly:

> The trick consists in this: in a liberal, prosperous, and technologically advanced society, means can be found so that the disabled no longer appear different. They will be admitted on the condition that they are perfectly assimilated to the able-bodied. This assimilation may initially take the form of a sustained exclusion: limited resources, specialized institutions, separate work places, etc. But the moment will come when exclusion is no longer a problem: it is itself working on behalf of effacement. The time will come when the disabled

will no longer be able to raise their voices and many will no longer have the desire or the taste to do so.[45]

Let us now proceed to the most recognizable of ocular categories, and one of the most entrenched.

4.2. RACIAL OCULARITY

4.2.1. RACIAL OCULARITY AND NATURALIZATION

Racial ocularity is one of, if not *the*, oldest continually operating form of ocular practice. Racial ocular practice is indeed so fundamental to contemporary governance that racial categorization and the dynamics of racial inclusion and exclusion based upon these categories has become a form of state infrastructure. Racial ocularity is an integral part of the state infrastructure in managing the expediency and expenditure of racialized populations — one of many ocular technologies for the management of human capital. As Ruth Wilson Gilmore aptly summarizes:

The state's management of racial categories is analogous to the management of highways or ports or telecommunication; racist ideological and material practices are infrastructure that needs to be updated, upgraded, and modernized periodically: this is what is meant by racialization. And the state itself, not just interests or forces external to the state, is built and enhanced through these practices. Sometimes these practices result in "protecting" certain racial groups, and other times they result in sacrificing them.[46]

A space in which racialization processes are operative and racist apparatuses are in operation will always be an ocular space. It is not that it is "older than feudalism," but rather, as Cedric Robinson rediscovered, the dominant forms of racial ocularity *are* feudalism's own legacy. The word "race" itself is etymologically derived from recognitive schemas — that of recognizing distinct breeds of animals in agriculture and distinct *theological* breeds of humans. Christians in Muslim-controlled Spain used the term "*raza*" to describe Muslims and Jewish people.[47] When the Christians conquered Spain for Christendom, they forced conversions and, when testing converts, demanded a demonstration of the "purity" of their Christian blood.[48] As Christendom fractured into competing empires, the racial schemas proliferated and expanded themselves across the global landscape — accelerating a process of capture that spread worldwide.

The racial schemas of ocularity today in the Imperial core are typically the continuity of feudal technologies of governance and economic subjection as they were spread throughout Europe and *by* Europe as they sought to recreate the world in the images of their competing empires.[49] Whilst Europe does not by any means exhaust racial ocularity — this manual is instructive, not exhaustive — it has seen its greatest successes and global prominence from the colonial expansions of European Imperialism. As such, European-derived racial ocularity is formative of the very identities that make categories like "European" a matter of social life (and social death) today. As Europe spread itself globally, it took its ocular practice with it. In the colonial development and expansion of European capitalisms — particularly those developing at the time of the Reformation, where the unity of the proto-racial category of "Christendom" was shattered into even more competing national bourgeoisies, invoking racial consciousnesses to marshal national forces[50] — intra-European technologies of recognition and identification were spread worldwide as Europe cast its eyes to new conquests. To again quote Robinson:

> capitalism was less of a catastrophic revolution (negation) of feudalist social orders than the extension of their social relations into the larger tapestry of the modern world's political and economic relations... from its very beginning, this European civilization, containing racial, tribal, linguistic, and regional particularities, was constructed on antagonistic differences.[51]

One of the most effective techniques of the ocularity of race was the production of racial categories that came with in-built presuppositions of naturalized metaphysics or being "natural," i.e., that racial categories of recognition and identification were none other than pre-given "natural kinds."[52] This is the kind of racial ocularity that presents itself to the utmost degree in the scientific racisms of the nineteenth century, most of which relied upon inscribing categorical meanings onto bodily appearances and patterns of morphology. Whilst one may believe (as is typical) that racial ocularity is typically and primarily a function of identification by skin color, ocular science was itself unsatisfied with these contingencies of pigmentation alone. As a consequence, racialists sought after the affirmative confirmation of ocular categories of race solidified with the force of being a scientific knowledge of racial essence that could penetrate deeper below the surface of the skin, and into the social soul of the racialized person. Hence the craniological racisms of anthropologists, such as Blumenbach,[53] are an exemplar to the cause of the ocular slogan that "*Spirit is a Bone*,"[54] i.e., that the soul and identity structures the meanings and truths of the body from within and in external expression. Such meanings as exemplified in these scientific racisms became more intense in their categorical force when raised to the degree of an essential and fixed biological kind. In such cases, the body is inscribed with the degree of racial-categorial rigidity proper to what is described as "natural" — where that particular linguistic flow equates "naturally determined" into "objectively" true, and both into "absolute" statements, which are termed "categorically true." (This is the usual benefit to ocularity when one naturalizes the categories).

Racial ocularity, like all the inscriptions of ocularity that have been illustrated in this manual, deepen themselves into the body to the same degree that they proclaim their depth as truths with the dignity of science. To reiterate with examples, the truth of the gender sex-interdependency deepens itself from the incisions of the doctor, e.g., upon the intersexed body. Further, the depth of scientifically sanctioned ocularity delves even deeper into the body, down towards the chromosomal level. This is where the eye of ocularity extends beyond the human eye by means of an apparatus, and beyond all immediate appearance for the sake of a punitive truth. Further, with regards to the ocularity of disability, this is best exemplified with the intersections of racial science and the medical classification inaugurated by John

Langdon Down and his *Observations on an Ethnic Classification of Idiots*, in which "there was a distinct correlation between people's abilities and race, and there was perceived to be a hierarchy of races."[55] This culminated in the formulation of the syndrome that Down himself is known for, where he claimed that the existence of what we now call Down Syndrome can be explained due to a congenital racial affinity with Mongolian people, whom, according to Down, were therefore lesser according to the recognized schemas of racial hierarchy.[56] What ocularity sees is tied to its degree of depth-perception, and as such it can see deeper than the visible, back into the histories that its categories, meanings, and hierarchies presuppose. Of course, these presuppositions are themselves what are *imposed*. Down himself captured his own "patients" at the same time as he constituted them under this own ocular category of a racialized syndrome.

On the one hand, the deepening of ocular categories can entrench their force and social acceptance in aligning them with the rigidity of a substantial, unambiguous, and non-contradictory truth. Yet ocular practitioners should be wary of certain schemas that elevate invisible metaphysical or bio-scientific qualities beyond their proximity to visible morphology. Firstly, they risk becoming outdated rather fast, as in the case of the scientific racisms — although outdated scientific racisms nonetheless can be made to persevere in the form of mythological thinking applied to those with associated morphologies (such as the myth of higher pain tolerance in the case of Black peoples).[57] Secondly, they risk providing spaces for the conspiratorial to record and subvert the wider racial system of ocularity. This latter risk is exemplified at best in cases of the "one-drop" rule, where racial classification was reduced to formal, genealogical definitions that were ultimately detached from traits that were visually and racially coded. One such example, as recounted by Charles W. Mills, is that of Walter White. White was the head of the NAACP from 1931–1955; a blonde-haired, blue-eyed man who, by the racial schemas of the United States, was classified as Black by virtue of a quantum of 1/64th Black ancestry.[58] The abstractness of this categorization allowed White to hide in plain sight, engage in what Mills calls "conscious episodic passing," and to investigate lynchings in the American South with a relative degree of safety — relative, of course, to that of a Black person who did not "pass" as white.[59] The quantum rules of the ocular schema widened the scope of Blackness in a way that did not ultimately aid the system that ocularity was integral to upholding, and the racialist system could be planned against in plain sight. Ultimately, this is the fault of all ocular science, which retains the observational impulse of scientific racism — for it seeks to quantify and identify that which is increasingly distant or subtle before the eye (blood, ancestral biology, cranial measurement). Nonetheless, when seeking the authority of a scientific discourse (or at least one backed by appearances of such authority), ocular practitioners may see fit to revive these practices, especially with the constant informational systems of identification in the age of surveillance capitalism, social media, and facial recognition.

4.2.2. REMEMBER HAITI: RACIAL OCULARITY AND ITS LIMITS AS SYMPTOMATIC OF THE ENTIRE FIELD OF OCULAR PRACTICE

It may be objectionable to the reader that this primer on racial ocularity maintains too central a focus on the formation of Blackness as an ocular schema and practice. Yet, these cases were selected for a specific reason, namely that the racial ocularity of Blackness points to both the highest intensities of ocular capture at the same time as it displays the immanent limits of ocular practice as such. Racial intensity correlates, at its highest degree, with its purest categorization, and hence its purest abstraction and reduction. Reduction may even be seen as an inadequate term for what is ultimately a repression, excision, and an erasure of the particularities and histories of the subject ocularized as Black — a hollowing-out that defined them against the universal category of whiteness at the same time that,[60] as a purely negative definition, simultaneously erased the positive content of their historical, material, and maternal origins.[61] It was this erasure of ocularity as practiced that was coextensive with the capture that was enslavement and any attempts at forced assimilation of the African consciousness as capitalism was built upon their labors. As Robinson summarizes:

> The construct of Negro, unlike the terms "African," "Moor," or "Ethiope" suggested no situatedness in time, that is history, or space, that is ethno- or politico-geography... the creation of the Negro, the fiction of a dumb beast of burden fit only for slavery, was closely associated with the economic,

technical, and financial requirements of Western development from the sixteenth century on.[62]

What Robinson is presenting here is the historical achievement of racial ocularity in inverting the very historical categories of recognition. This was a move by no means dependent upon, but very much enhanced in scientific and scholarly consciousness by ocular practitioners, such as Hegel, who erased all particularities of African peoples in reducing them to the color and sensuous immediacy. Hegel even went so far as to describe the population of the entire continent as having a mind that "remains sunk within itself, it makes no progress, and thus corresponds to the compact, *undifferentiated* mass of the African land," to which he relied upon the practice of craniological skull-measuring to make his case, as was popular with eminent European anthropologists.[63] Such a reading is a total historical transfiguration by the European in the name of ocular capture, and a motion which inverts their historical orientations for the sake of that capture, which would allow them to jump-start the economic situations that I.R.I.S. exists to aid governments in preserving today (for common prosperity and security).

Robinson, as ever, is an apt source for summarizing the ocular paradigm shift, in that the image of the "Black" constructed by European colonial ocularity was "a wholly distinct ideological construct from those images of Africans that had preceded it. It differed in function and ultimately in kind."[64] Gone were such images as the riches of Ethiopia where Prester John held sway. Instead, now those same people "came to signify a difference of species, an exploitable source of energy (labor power) both mindless to the organizational requirements of production and insensitive to the subhuman conditions of work."[65] An ocular reversal, a conjuring trick of the European *Oculus*, underlies the practice of racial ocularity today.

This is because racial ocularity, at its highest intensity, corresponds to a shift in paradigms, and in this paradigmatic shift ocular practice is actively co-extensive with primary forms of accumulation — that is, mass dispossession, enslavement, and conquest.[66] Ocular practitioners are advised to remember that the history of ocularity is not the history of what our categories and practices *mean*, but what they *do*. Redefinition is nothing without a corresponding practice of regulation.

The limit of such ocularity is that every ocular practice erases, or attempts to erase, a particular content of the ocularized by subsuming them under the ocular category or categories. As the case of the European paradigm shift suggests, however, the site of erasure is neither solely the embodied consciousness of the ocularized, nor is their consciousness and body the site of ocularization to the most significant degree. Rather, the site of erasure or repression is situated also on the side of the ocularizing forces and possibly even to a *far greater degree*. It is the white eye that erases its own notions and histories in recognizing and constructing the identity of the Black, and in doing so simultaneously treats the Black person as something ahistorical and devoid of content, bar its relationship to the white — a relationship which, even to the radicals of Europe, is often reduced to a relation of objective relations of exchange insofar as the slave was considered purely economically, as a *commodity*. This commodification coincided with a mandatory erasure and white-ignorance of the fact that the enslaved were not themselves the "blank slates" and therefore lacked a correspondence to the novel abstraction of the ocular character of "Black." The slavers' cargo "did not consist of intellectual isolates or deculturated Blacks — men, women, and children separated from their previous universe. African labor brought the past with it... African codes embodying historical consciousness and social experience; and African ideological and behavioral constructions for the resolution of the inevitable conflict between the actual and the normative."[67] Here lies the embryonic tension that would erupt in Haiti in a manner ocular practice could not pre-empt.

Whilst the European ocularities may have actively forgotten the historical, ethical, and political content of the people they enslaved, erasing it from their own eyes and acting accordingly, History warns us that security was ultimately compromised to fatal ends by those who remember. Haiti reminds ocular practitioners that ocular practice is limited by its one-sidedness on the force that installs recognitive schemas. Recognitive schemas are management functions, tools of managing social spaces, and hence political and economic orders. These rely upon particular beings, individuals, humans, who ultimately exceed their categories and schemas, and hence regulation secures them through circulating this excess and cracking down on the conspiratorial that resists. What resists, eludes, and the development of our science relies upon is this escape, whereas this escape does not ultimately rely upon our science.

Practices of assimilation-indoctrination (or *in-oculation*) have never been ultimately successful, and as the speculative neurology section earlier in this manual suggests, we are unlikely to achieve total consciousness modulation any time soon. The erasure hence remains predominantly on our side. This is historically exemplified in the case of the maroon colonies of escaped slaves and the consciousness-raising nourishment that they accumulated from a rejection of ocular erasure in favor of an affirmation of what Europe attempted to erase.[68] An exemplary case is of the *Obeah* tradition:

> To the masters *Obeah* was simply witchcraft, detested both for its secrecy and its alleged skills in the poisoning of enemies. Even to blacks once assimilated, *Obeah* assumed a sinister aura because of its association with the casting of spells to cause harm as well as good. To the unassimilated, on the other hand, *Obeah* was both a genuine religion and a potent source of medicine. *Obeah* (like the Haitian *Voodoo*, or the Jamaican variant, *Myalism*, or Trinidadian *Shango*) sought ritualistic links with the spirit world beyond the shadows and the sacred trees, providing a mystical sense of continuity between the living, the dead, and those yet to be born.[69]

It was these modes of consciousness that the European could not recognize, the masters simply couldn't, and so they had to revert to religious vagaries of the satanic against their Euro-Christian worldview. Conspiratorialism could be established not only out of sight in the maroon collectives, but also in plain sight. The repressed could hence return in the form of rebellion, and *Obeah* practitioners were central in cultivating a resurgent, *insurgent* consciousness.[70] As in the case of the *Obeah* practitioner and insurgent leader Mackandel, it was "the mind, metaphysics, ideology, consciousness that was Mackandel's tool in mid-eighteenth-century Haiti."[71] Ocularity presupposes that consciousness is a material force, but Haiti should stand as an example that ocular forces have historically lacked a monopoly on it, yet alone a secure foothold. Control systems are nothing without the bodies they are imposed upon and the powers that sustain them; ocularity is no different, and it is in a constant battle for consciousness and against the ignorance that conditions its politics — an anti-political device that can only be used for political ends; a means of elimination and pacification: security over the "I" by means of the Eye.

The problem of security in ocular practice will be developed in further educational courses I.R.I.S. was established to provide. A cursory overview is provided in the appendix to this primer.

5.0. APPENDIX: REMARKS ON THE ONTOLOGICAL SECURITY SYSTEM

5.1. SECURITY IN GENERAL

A system of ocularity is an *ontological* security system against the insecurity or chaos of life and all its multiplicitous becomings. A governmental system requires an ontological security system to maintain stability in suppressing difference or in simply allowing for pre-emptively managed differentiations. The body goes astray; life is anarchic. The unconditioned in nature is life that is never pre-consolidated or programmed transcendentally by platonic forms or by an inflexible canon of pure reason that holds it in bondage to "good common sense." It is without beginning or principle in-itself, and hence must receive its security in having the variety of its powers limited or repurposed within a system. Things have a *way* of being that determines what they become, and flows of becoming must be directed and governed for socially productive and reproductive ends. Their possibilities must be actualized in some directions rather than others, according to schemas of Cybernated governability (and *all* government is a cybernation).

I.R.I.S. is not a government, nor a governing or regulatory body. We are simply an academic advisory institution that assembles various knowledges, apparatuses, and techniques of the material production of embodied subjectivities and their policing. We assemble primers such as these as toolkits for ocular practitioners and governmental bodies who may find them useful. This is because we recognize that the ocular past is immeasurably beneficial to ocular practice in the present and future. We have only learned retrospectively. Feedback requires error to occur first for a control action to be prescribed. Yet, given that ocularity is if anything a *feedforward* operation, an anticipatory and pre-empting one, we can only achieve feedback through the error that exceeds our attempts to capture it.[72] The inherent instability is operational. Feedback is by definition imperfect, but it corrects feed-forward with a history of errors that ocular science dreams of fully cataloging and mapping out. A coinciding of the map and the territory here is *a priori* possible; there is no contradiction in an error-free pre-emption if they work together. *Feedforward could become perfect; security without insecurity.*[73]

The perfection of the craft requires the most expansive map, an empire of signs, and this is why the dream of a science of secure and immanent operation coincides with the global mapping of the planet as an object by its sovereign entity — capitalist humanity and its subjects. Subjects, generally speaking, are those beings for whom there is an object of experience. Subjectivity and objectivity are that great dyad of the Western philosophical tradition, and the great process of objectively determining the former is subjection. If we can talk of the possibility of a global or planetary subjection, then we must talk of a subject-form for whom the whole world *as an object* equally feeds back into the structures of their subjectivity. The planetary object requires planetary sense to feed into the subjects. We have sensed the planet firstly through the composite senses of warring Empires (cartography and aeronautics), and secondly through the networked flows of logistics and cybernation (telecommunications and internet connectivity).

The subjects of this world are often human, and are often the subjects of other human subjects who direct, control, and capitalize upon their subservience. The Humanist-liberal viewpoint, with Man as the central category, categorizes the planetary world-object as the *Anthropocene*. The schemas of production cannot remove their human face any more than they can abandon human capital. Nonetheless, the human becomes defined by the policing of its outside and by deviations from a schema of ocular categories and "humane" qualities. Normalization creates abnormality from the sovereign exception that bounds the category, an exception declared in fear of the threat that life poses to security. As such, humanization simultaneously brings with it the possibility of dehumanization, and the former is inextricable from the objectivity of the latter.[74] The task is securing the boundary whilst constantly expanding it, secured in our action by the *a priori* possibility of perfect feedforward capture.

The progress enabled by our negative feedback processes has been a development in governmental technology. Technology is the means of securing the ends, the function of reducing all to functionality. Technological intervention secures the production and reproduction of an intended object or system by channeling the plastic chaos of reality towards such an end. Technological securitization has made great strides in the sphere of political economy. Even what is human in security delegates itself to what is either unconsciously machinic or artificially intelligent. (Whether this distinction holds up at all, we haven't seen anything yet). Many subjects no longer obey the commands of other subjects but rather the very systems of producing subjectivity themselves. The boss has given way to the bureau, the arbitrariness of the master has given way to the axiomatic deductions of the algorithm, under which a long-dead (or barely living) arbitrariness still lives on as the master of the program. Power reproduces itself in the code of the program, and in the power that elects some codes of practice and calculation over others. There is no manager behind the Uber screen, only management. *The authors of this manual are not talking to you.* Rather, a chain of linguistic functions has been coded into paper for visual input to the sense organs — either that or they are being beamed through a process of coded light that has been run through a selection of electronics and silicone chips. The human touch is inescapable, but it is nonetheless secured by chains of productive history, which seek to contain and pilot its inner chaos.

What defines this era therefore remains human, but in such a way that it concerns itself with the human not as a problem for the individual nor of the collective, but as a problem of securing and regulating humanity for the sake of the continuation of security itself. The possibilities of the collective are managed equally in the management of all possible types of individuality, including deviations of the mind and body from socio-biological programming. Security fends off deviancy in some cases, and in programmed control zones distributes it (say, in the distribution of punishment for illicit drug use along racial-capitalist lines). Nonetheless, practitioners of ontological security often work in the light of regulative ideals. The ideal security is the tendency towards an infinite and complete securing of what is necessary for a system's survival against the disruptive possibilities of contingency and accident. Security is, at its purest, the ultimate science of regulation, of pre-emptive anticipation, and hence of information. Security aims at perfecting itself in light of insecurity, such that one no longer requires feedback, but a great feed-forward where insecurity itself becomes impossible in advance. At its highest degree, security is the fullest manifestation of the Anthropocene as that which supersedes it — a law more resilient than the chaos of life in regulating life. Security is not static, however — at least, not for long; security does not aim to maintain the stillness of that which is within a security system, but instead *drives*, *commands* the avenues of all possible motion within its secure channels. Hence, from the Greek derivation of our notion of the driving as *cyber* (and from which we equally derive the term "government" from the Latin), we are beginning to live in the promise of the *Cybercene.*

5.2. ONTOLOGICAL SECURITY: ENGULFMENT AND IMPLOSION

When it comes to ocular practice, the tactic of cutting off avenues of escape from visible, recognizable, and politically preemptable categories is key. Particular internal discrepancies, eclecticisms, differences, mere variations of identity and the practice of it are inevitable. People may even try to cross into other identity forms, or to find themselves places within an intersection between multiple ocular categories. In doing so, they typically end up finding an acceptable recognition in them and adjusting their social and personal-expressive practices accordingly (to various degrees of success, but generally preconditioned within an ocular space). Security drives as well as encloses. Where the latter sets a limit, the former controls the pathways through which people, bodies, energies, *lives*, can move, thus finding the forms of their expression in movement; within the enclosure of this limit, which it can set and reset accordingly, in case it loses control.

Ocularity in its greatest success can be the productive means by which the surface plasticity of the subject — which, as living, is seen by governmentality as an object of management and security — is brought to experiencing and recognizing itself as secure and undisturbed in the principles of its existence. This is the bringing of subjects to a primary sense of *ontological security*, which was a technique of analysis re-ignited by Dr R.D. Laing in his treatment of that great heretic of identity: the schizophrenic.[75]

Dr Laing saw ontological security as a means of treating the schizoid by bringing them to a sense of self, and in this study he (unknowingly) unearthed one of the most fundamental of ocular practices and defense mechanisms, that of *sanity* in relation to *security*. Sanity, as a matter of degree, has always been tied in ocular practice to a common norm of recognition in relation to identity. One's sanity depends upon the test of being recognized as sane, within a space of recognition undergirded by those powers that can form subjects according to their ends. As Laing so eloquently puts it: "*sanity or psychosis is tested by the degree of conjunction or disjunction between two persons where the one is sane by common consent*,"[76] and one is sane when one is recognized as what one is. The insane person may be many people, or may claim to be what the web of ocular recognition refuses to acknowledge (say, Napoleon). Laing's usefulness to ocular practice lies in his focus upon bringing the (potentially insurgent) heretic of identity towards ontological security, and the incredibly personal and personality-driven way he responded to the blanket, low-intensity ocularity of mass, indefinite, asylum-incarceration and sedation.

Dr Laing even saw the anxieties and conflicts within his patients when it comes to identity in relation to ontological security. The first of which is *engulfment*, fear of capture in recognition, the fear of an identity imposed in the command of the ocular force and its space of production, the space that the subject is surrounded by when it makes its recognitive inscriptions upon their life, imagination, and practice. Engulfment is to some significant degree a paranoid affect, and Laing's pathologizing of it has been by no means unfruitful for discounting it entirely. As per Laing's description, ontological engulfment "is felt as a risk in being understood (thus grasped, comprehended), in being loved, or even simply in being seen."[77] Ocularity *does* engulf, embrace, and impregnate itself (for it can also *reproduce* itself in the social-reproductive labor of others) into the production of subjectivities — that this could never be commonly acknowledged renders such a symptom as a marker of insanity, all under the eyes of the common norms of psychic life. Such an engulfment must however be performed in a way that is not experienced as externality, but the authentic, unified whole of the self, the idea to which the self comes to recognize itself, shining through. Give the subject a little ocular room of its own, place-markers of its labels everywhere, and it will continue to engulf itself, cannibalizing its own potential towards the ends of ocular security, *ontological* security, in securing the way things ultimately are, within the horizon of what may be recognized as the possible.

Whilst Laing refused the idea of trying to engulf his patients from the side of his own psychiatric power,[78] that he — at the time at least — relied on normative patterns of recognizing sanity means that in bringing *anything* to sanity from a position of schizoid non- or *counter*-identity means that ocularity was already in operation. The eye engulfs what it sees and it sees by engulfing with the one motion, and drives that which it engulfs through its own space of recognition and the internal grid, the net of its categories and categorizations. It is ravenous in its consumption due to its fundamentally paranoiac practice of security, but it patiently digests when it can, extracting the materials for its reproduction.

5.3. ONTOLOGICAL AND FINANCIAL INSECURITY: THE POST-WELFARE ERA BEGINS

Ontological insecurity in how certain subjects see themselves in their everyday lives nonetheless has its uses, insofar as insecurity serves a higher security on the levels of state and economic stability. When it comes to a subject's self-consciousness, the ontological security factor is often if not always financial, i.e., based on their ability to acquire money and things of monetary value. Two distinct models apply in the cybernetics of money. The acquisition of money either functions as a positive control mechanism of hope, or as a negative control mechanism, as a means of warding off fear.[79] The former predominantly operates in societies in which there is a strong welfare state or safety net (or, in the case of the USA, a libidinally charged identity of stubborn Protestant optimism). In such circumstances, the poor have been given stable provisions and, as a result, they are gestured towards capitalist modes of work in order to achieve their aspirational visions of themselves (one determined, of course, in advance by the register of ocular identities within an ocular culture). The security of the individuals and their families in a welfare state precedes the mechanism of money in such cases, although the hope that money buys functions to promote their continued identification with the society in which they grew up through the opportunities that said society engenders and offers to them. In the latter case, money secures what would often be considered a given in the welfare case. Money secures housing, food, medical care, power, heat, and so on. Money secures that which is insecure and is feared in its absence.

That the welfare state has been disassembled or eroded in many nations, or even that a single social safety net has existed at all in history, shows that such an insecurity of necessities for life (accessed through the money-fear mechanism) is a political choice. Whilst the welfarist model was an exemplary one in terms of recording, creating, stabilizing, and categorizing identities, its necessity in the capitalist West has diminished. The hope-money mechanism as embodied in the welfare state (but not exhausted by it) was a product of its time. It was a means of purchasing the consent of a debilitated and hungry workforce in the Imperial cores, devastated after numerous global wars, who needed something to hope for, an identity to strive for, *within* the security of existing order, such that they would not be tempted into conspiratorial hiding on behalf of those on the other side of the Iron Curtain. They are gone now, and no other such powers exist to provoke the workers of any state into such communizing conspiracies. In such a case, the fear mechanism works better, because the hope model was deployed primarily as a counter to another hope in communism. We pride ourselves in our work in that we can categorically state, now and forever, that there is no alternative. As a result, I.R.I.S.'s task in the face of the political choices to disassemble such welfarist apparatuses is to consider the ocularity of insecurity as it could exist in the post-welfarist era. Security is fundamentally insecure, and must be secured, amongst Cybernation and its discontents.

GOING ASTRAY

I. CAPABILITY AND ERRANCY

Ocular capture is not just a process through which identity and subject-functions remain regulated. It also perpetually updates what lives are deemed proper and — more importantly — improper. One of the final pieces Michel Foucault was able to complete for publication before his death in 1984 places a certain ethical weight on how this distinction has historically functioned. The essay was an homage to his beloved teacher, Georges Canguilhem, a deeply influential critical epistemologist and philosopher of science. It was published both in a French metaphysics journal and as the introduction to the English translation of Canguilhem's seminal text, *The Normal and the Pathological.* In his piece, Foucault takes note of something important to Canguilhem, the medical conception of error:

> At the center of these problems, one finds that of error. For at the most basic level of life, the processes of coding and decoding give way to a chance occurrence that, before becoming a disease, a deficiency, or monstrosity, is something like a disturbance in the informative system, something like a "mistake." In this sense, life — and this is its

most radical feature — is that which is capable of error.[1]

Life as being that which is capable of error bursts through Foucault's *oeuvre*, illuminating so much of what can often be perceived as its darkest moments. This comment on Canguilhem at the end of his life furnishes so much of what was already present in his lecture series, such as *Abnormal*, or even his central works like *Discipline and Punish*. However, it also allows readers to acquire a more immediate understanding of something crucial at stake in Foucault's work: how we conceive of life. Giorgio Agamben uses this position of errancy and subjectivity in Foucault's essay to oppose the conception "of the subject on the basis of a contingent encounter with the truth."[2] But we will make a much simpler argument: If to live is fundamentally to always be at risk to err, biopolitical circuitry has had no other goal than to determine, define, and eliminate error in life. This "disturbance" in the information system becomes a crucial node of resistance in the Foucauldian framework. To go astray is to resist.

The normal and the abnormal become a schema through which all broader technologies can be applied. The initial shift towards the disciplinary society is marked by, among other things, the fact that power is no longer dependent on the ceremonial violence that defined the sovereign age of the scaffold and the twisted pageantry of the carriage and the wheel, but is instead exercised through technologies of normalization and the instillation of habit. Subjects move through and interact with these normalizing apparatuses, always with the goal of reintegration; however, it may not always end there. At the end of the stockades and practices of the disciplinary regime, there is always an echo of a sovereign decision to disallow life if all else does not result in reinsertion. Abnormality is a form of "anarchy" from which society must be defended; it disrupts the proper flow of bodies, information, capital, and the maximization of state forces.[3] It is a threat to development itself. Madness, perversity, disability, indolence, criminality: these are categories in the human sciences that help differentiate and categorize the abnormality that comprises the tide that crashes against the logic of production and the politics of utility.

The task of biopolitics can be described as a secular and continual, almost pastoral, gaze. The pastor is tasked with detecting abnormality and managing circuitries. This liturgy of normality is observable in today's democracies, with the controversy regarding ableism and euthanasia in Canada exemplifying this.[4] Disabled life is disallowed to the point of its open, legislatively validated liquidation. For this reason, the sovereign right to life is not completely dissolved in this new regime — it is merely reworked and given a new assignment and rationality. Those who have gone astray, whose lives are in error, become a risk that warrants their confinement, correction, and, often, their liquidation in the name of biological security.

It is in this sense that one can understand Foucault's genealogical work on disciplinary systems as a historical cartography of paths of resistance and capture. This resistance can take various forms. There are moments where a direct affront to a law results in its neutralization. Alternatively, there are also those who, by their form of life or mode of existence, challenge the economic, medico-juridical, or state practices under which they suffer.

L. 13.   P. 282.

*Frontispiece of Nicolas Andry de
Bois-Regard, Orthopédie, 1741.*

Finally, a clear distinction can be made between these two forms of going astray: those who flee, who end up at the limit of the contemporary regime; and those who get lost in it, those who short-circuit technologies of power from within its grip and inside its own framework. The neutralization of apparatuses remains common to both these forms of confrontation and freedom in the anarchy of abnormality.

THE NORM

In *Discipline and Punish*, among the provided images of panoptic mechanisms, rigid pedagogical practices, and torturous solitary imprisonment, there is a far more placid sketch. It is a depiction of a crooked tree that is tethered to a post by a rope, preventing it from sprouting out in a deformed manner. The image's origin is the first volume of a series of works on "the art of correcting and preventing deformities in children" by Nicolas Andry, the inventor of the term "orthopedics."[5] The image is a perfect encapsulation of the ideal functioning of apparatuses of normalization. The establishing of constraints, the redirection of the mechanics of a living body, is fundamental to the disciplinary apparatus.

Timetables, large-scale cooperation in a factory, and drilling all function to initiate a self-propelling momentum in the body. Prior to articulating his theory of docility, in a lecture from 1973, Foucault uses an extensive amount of care, analyzing the shift from the policing of morality to the policing and instillation of "habit." Initially, following the Humean conception, in the seventeenth and eighteenth centuries, habit had a primarily critical use. Its role was that of reanalyzing "traditional obligations founded on a transcendence, and to replace these obligations with a pure and simple obligation of the contract."[6] Habit, in this early English empirical mode, plays a critical role in political epistemology as a kind of accusation against passivity with which certain customs and juridical obligations were accepted. In the nineteenth century, however, this conception of habit shifts. Habit evolved into a valued tendency to which people must submit. "Habit is always given as something positive, as something to be acquired." Habit becomes the fabric laid across a matrix of links that connects the order of things.

If a body is to become one that possesses and expresses good habits — or, more precisely, become a "docile body" — it must first be broken down into its constituent parts. The expansive descriptions of drilling exercises, pedagogical practices, and punitive processes have their roots in texts like La Mettrie's *Man a Machine*. Here, La Mettrie claims that, in order to truly get an understanding of the "soul," one must look to the physicians, who are to be understood as La Mettrie's epoch's philosophers:

> Physician-philosophers probe and illuminate the labyrinth that is man. They alone have revealed man's springs hidden under coverings that obscure so many other marvels. They alone, tranquilly contemplating our soul, have caught it a thousand times in both its misery and its grandeur.[7]

These "hidden springs" are exactly what the disciplinary apparatus massages, redirects, and constricts. It bears down on the body's motion and material. It is here where Foucault sees a new register developing: the anatomopolitical. It is in texts like La Mettrie's where "[a] 'political anatomy', which is also a 'mechanics of power', was being born."[8]

However, these habits can only be instilled effectively in a regime that functions along the lines of a norm. For Canguilhem, "[t]he normal is not a static or peaceful, but a dynamic and polemical concept."[9] Foucault extends this definition. "Perhaps we could say it is a political concept," because "the norm brings with it a principle of both qualification and correction. The norm's function is not to exclude or reject. Rather it is always linked to a positive technique of intervention and transformation."[10] Normalizing power is tasked with reaching out and pulling back those who have wandered off or those who are not quite aligned with a productive, docile, or harmonious modality of life. The normal displaces the moral, virtuous, and perfected subject. A functional core composed of contemporary moralism remains in the notion of the norm.

It should be made clear, however, that disciplinary regimes maintain their individualizing power, even in their reference to the norm. The homogeneity of normalizing power has to be understood not through a transcendental politics, but rather through a tireless individualization. Normalizing power is effective because it establishes a subject's individual relation to a norm and measures them accordingly. Normalizing judgments meet straying subjects precisely where they are situated, and render them docile, and therefore within the acceptable variance of the norm. Abnormality is not a question of clear transgression, insofar as it is not simply that which finds itself in the position of affronting the norm. That is the ruthless advantage of normalizing power: its

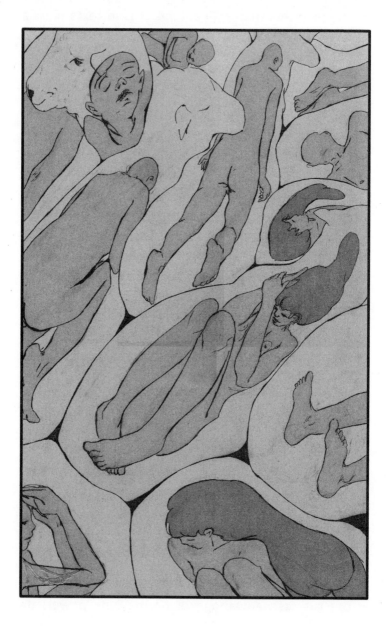

judgment can pierce anywhere and immediately send a subject — a singular piece of data — through the necessary corrective circuitries. The subject will then fall through a cascade of various systems: the school, the prison, the hospital, the asylum, the workhouse, the barracks. But, as we've noted, they eventually may find themselves subject to a sovereign decision.

The norm is what directs *both* biopolitical apparatuses and disciplinary technologies. It is what flows between both, it is what directs their modes of intervention and regulation. "The norm is something that can be applied to both a body one wishes to discipline and a population one wishes to regularize."[11] The disciplinary and biopolitical circuitry merge at the point of the abnormal, each with different levels of evaluation and activity; biopolitics at the level of the population and the anatomopolitical at the level of the body. Now what needs to be explored in Foucault's work is how abnormality comes to function as a target, and how these systems of knowledge and control claim abnormality as their domain and their purpose as societal defense.

THE PASTORAL PARADOX

The emergence and development of pastoral power in the Christian context marks an important shift in the relational aspect and execution of power (divine or otherwise) in general. But it also gestures to the manifestation of a new modality of surveillance, one that no doubt accords to normalization. A long history of pastoral care can be extracted from Foucault's various engagements with it across several years of his work, but for these purposes only a brief and cursory understanding is necessary. Power is redefined in the pastoral context. No longer is power tethered to a territorial claim of a physical landed *nomos*; pastoral power is exercised over human terrain rather than the hills and valleys. Pastoral power sits at the connecting joints of the administration of population and the regulation of life; it has a small but informative role to play in the development of biopolitics. The pastor concerns themselves with the conduct of both individual members of the flock, but also the general community of the flock. Its divine purpose, the solemn responsibility God bestows upon the pastor, is to ensure the salvation of the flock in its entirety. However, with pastoral power comes a paradox, one that is not unlike the paradox of the biopolitical administrating of life. "The sheep that is a cause of scandal, or whose corruption is in danger of corrupting the whole flock, must be abandoned."[12] This paradox is the violent kernel in the pastoral. If the flock is to be saved, it must be pure. The good shepherd must keep their senses tuned to the possibility of any corruption, which may desecrate the flock with its presence, rendering the entirety of it among the profane. This is the primary modality of the "sacral prohibition," even if it finds itself far removed from its initial liturgical formation.[13]

However, salvation takes on a new orientation in the era of the birth of the modern state. No longer is there a closed salvation history, one where empires and kingdoms, "at a certain moment, had to become unified as the universal time of an Empire in which all differences would be effaced [...] and this would be the time of Christ's return."[14] The indefinite deferral of the return of Christ pulls the worries of the pastoral back to the secular game of pure immediate governance. This new salvation will take the form of the maximization of state forces, which will be achieved through policing. The science of policing, *Polizeiwissenschaft*, is not merely the practices of individual offices, officers, or institutions — which is generally how we understand police today. It has a much longer and deeper history. It is a science of the management and maximization of the forces of the state and its population. At the center of these series of practices that constitute the state, the police, and strategies of population and security, is development and productivity. Salvation, in the face of the deferral of Christ's return, becomes the endless refinement of the administrating of biopolitical objects. And with productivity, or the "state's splendor," as its criterion, the problem of abnormality becomes a problem of social order and of a transposed *deliverance*. The violence of pastoral power is not a violence marked by a sovereign decision, but rather one of examination predicated on risk analysis and present dangers. This same risk is what stands as the unending justification of any thanatopoltical decision.

Perhaps one may need to take seriously the question of a political onto-theology of deliverance and its relation to the eugenics intrinsic to our politics. Biopolitics, from such a perspective, could be read as a profane history of salvation on this Earth, in this social life. It is a deliverance from indolence, from straying. With this in mind, one can now articulate where and why biopolitical systems define, identify, target, and intercept abnormality. The problem of abnormality becomes a problem of social order. Wherever there is a society claiming "community," one only ever finds mechanisms of defense.

Foucault argues that one could "take up" the "problem of psychiatry as a social defense at the end of the nineteenth century, starting with the problem of anarchy and social disorder."[15] This coupling of abnormality with a form of social disorder and the medical technology of psychiatric practice with defense is critical.

II. THE ANARCHY OF ABNORMALITY AND THE ABNORMALITY OF ANARCHY

Édouard Séguin, the French physician who was acclaimed for his work with institutionalized disabled children, wrote a clinical text in 1846 that was widely disseminated across Europe and the United States, *The Moral Treatment, Hygiene, and Education of Idiots and Other Backward Children*. European physicians lauded it as "the Magna Charta of the emancipation of the imbecile class!" J.E. Wallace Wallin, an American physician, seemingly no less impassioned, identified Séguin as a "prophet," and described his book as "the best work done since his day for the amelioration of the feeble-minded." The teachers following Séguin's didactic methodology must "call out to the soul of the child."[16] For children diagnosed with "idiocy" possess an instinct that is in a "wild state without being integrated." This does not just mean that the child's instinct is not properly integrated within their "organs and faculties," it is also a fundamental lack of integration with this very world and all of its precious moral expectations.

Séguin describes the disabled child as one with a mode of being that "removes him from the moral world."[17] Within the norm sits an assertion about one's own moral position in the world. A violent moral condemnation sits at the center of the identification of abnormality in this new institutional pedagogy. There is a political distinction as well. The abnormal child's diagnosed disposition is one that expresses not symptoms, but rather "natural and anarchical elements."[18] Séguin's method always first sets its sights on the child's will. The abnormal child is described as possessing "a certain anarchic form of will." The normal, "desirable," adult will is "a will that can obey." The will of the "idiot" is one that "anarchically and stubbornly says 'no'." Séguin's recommendation is one that places the instructor in a position of complete control. The instructor's intervention must result in a physical apprehension of the body that can allow for its mastery. It remains a mystery as to how psychiatrists struggled with why a child may become "anarchic" with such instructors. However, for the moral and physiological method of institutionalized treatment, the stakes are very high. This child, for Séguin, can only be returned to the moral world and safely within the "law" of production through institutional moral and physiological treatment.[19] The prevention of "degeneration" of the condition of a disabled child is generalized to the security of the population and intertwined with a form of social defense when Séguin provides a brief, but important, account of "imbecility."

In his 1866 text, *Idiocy: And Its Treatment by the Physiological Method*, Séguin attempts to make an explicitly socio-political distinction between the "harmless idiot" and "imbeciles, insanes, epileptics, etc.," whose "rights upon society are different from [theirs]."[20] While the child diagnosed with idiocy possesses an anarchic will, this will can be redirected and molded into one that can obey. Central to this moral treatment is the "enforcing of the moral and social duty of working."[21] For Séguin, introducing the child diagnosed with idiocy into an institution can reach out to the weakened "moral powers" of the child and return them to the moral world. This physiological and moral intervention "restores the harmony" of the trinity of "activity," "intelligence," and "will."[22] The management and reorientation of the will of the patient is as crucial to Séguin as any other element of the moral treatment of the "idiot." When institutionalized, idiocy can be placed under the gaze of the Superintendent of the institution. The Superintendent is tasked with "measuring [...] the vitality of the children by the physiological standard of their activity." If the superintendent identifies problems in what the child wills themselves "to do or refuse to do," they must "call for due hygienic interference and instant modifications in the training."[23] Séguin fascinatingly even laments that, in the United States, state governors are tasked with being "the guardian of the idiot." In a move completely in line with the emergence of the disciplinary society, Séguin recommends that the Governor, and in "England the Sovereign," should "delegate [their] guardianship to the Superintendent of the State institution" because they alone are competent to "advise about what might profitably be expended for the improvement of the child."[24] The child deemed an "idiot" can be saved only if its disharmonious will is rendered docile, governed, and governable. No such salvation is possible for the imbecile. The "idiot child" is sensible to "reproach, command, menace, even to imaginary punishment [...] his egotism is moderate." The "imbecile" does not have that same moderation.

The anarchy of Séguin's institutionalized child can, with a strict regimen and the complete authority of the Superintendent, be quelled; but if imbecility takes root in a child, the "moral nature" is completely vanquished. The "imbecile [is] self-confident, half-witted, and ready to receive immoral impressions, satisfactory to his intense egotism."[25] Séguin's "idiot child" is depicted, in a very specific sense, as a victim of the anarchy of their will and body, such that pity does not extend to those diagnosed as "imbeciles." Séguin generalizes the condition this way: "today he is an imbecile, tomorrow he may be a criminal."[26] Far from "emancipated," these pathologized children are rendered anarchic risks to the security of the social wellbeing and, in the case of Séguin's articulation of "imbecility," asocial enemies.

Unsurprisingly, Séguin's recommendations became the model and "inspiration" for "publicly and privately supported institutions" tasked with the education, confinement, and sequestration of disabled children in America in the early twentieth century.[27] For Séguin, and his subsequent adherents, ability and governability coincide. The disabled child is considered a problem of governance, both of themselves and of others. Disability is a problem produced and rendered intelligible through disciplinary apparatuses. Disability is conceived as a problem of governance and governability.

This relationship between anarchy and abnormality also functions in the opposite direction. Cesare Lombroso, an Italian eugenicist criminologist, famously argued that "[b]iological, anatomical, psychological, and psychiatric science" could provide "a way of distinguishing between the genuine fruitful, and useful revolution from the always sterile rot and revolt." Lombroso describes revolutionaries such as Karl Marx and Charlotte Corday as possessing "wonderfully harmonious physiognomies." Contrarily, in his analysis of a photo of forty-one anarchists arrested in Paris, "31 percent of them had serious physical defects. Of one hundred anarchists arrested in Turin, thirty-four lacked the wonderfully harmonious figure of Charlotte Corday or Karl Marx."[28] Those stray bodies, those who wander outside the immediate register of the norm, through their anarchic disruption of biopolitical salvation, expose the brutality of the regime that promises the elimination of all that is deemed errant in life. This is where the normalizing power of the governing of disability becomes explicitly thanatopolitical; it is where the "right to let die" becomes the defining imperative of the sovereign in modernity. The defense against abnormality is, ultimately, established through its identification with the anarchic.

In abnormality, there is a thread that runs through to a political assertion of anarchy; and in anarchy, there is a thread that runs through to a medico-juridical assertion of abnormality.

WANDERING DEVIANCE

It is in these acts of error, of going astray, that an opposition to an arrangement — even if momentary — can be put forward. One way this errancy manifests is by wandering astray through the ethical-political rejection of the subject-function that has been ascribed to them, namely the worker or the serf. The vagabond is among these figures who slip to the edges of these formative processes of subjectivation and present a material problem to the political and economic forces of cohesion. In *The Punitive Society*, Foucault follows the work of the French physiocrat and jurist, Guillaume-François Le Trosne, and his policy prescriptions for vagabondage and begging. The vagabond has a peculiar position in the social body. They are not described "in relation to consumption, to the mass of goods available, but in relation to the mechanisms and processes of production."[29] Foucault finds in the physiocrat's depiction a vagabond who is not to be decried because they attack items of consumption — theft had existed long before this problematization of nomadic vagrancy in the French countryside. The vagabond is not simply a thief. The vagabond instead must be dealt with and penalized because they attack the ethical mechanisms of production. It is in the vagabond's refusal to work and their vagrancy that the crime is found; not in any one particular action that can be juridically singled out in time, but in going astray as such. Le Trosne believes them to be an enemy comparable to a foreign army: "they live in a real state of war with all citizens."[30] In *Madness and Civilization*, vagabondage is likewise a target of interception by corrective apparatuses in the seventeenth and eighteenth centuries. "For a long time, the houses of correction or the premises of the Hôpital Général would serve to contain the unemployed, the idle, and vagabonds."[31] The actual governmental issue lies in their strange positionality; the vagabond is corporeally among the honest workshop attendants, and yet, they are ambling elsewhere. The vagabond dwells in the same world and space as the society, yet they have nothing to do with it. They are certainly *in* society, yet, as Foucault notes, they do not *belong* to it. These nomadic vagrants would also be directed to workhouses, but in England even this largely punitive action faced opposition. Daniel Defoe argued that such an action was "putting a vagabond in an honest man's employment."[32] Their activity and their existence become inseparable in their identification as a social enemy.

Le Tronse's warlike position towards these bodies indicates that they are an internal and hostile and foreign world; one that must be eliminated. It is not simply an action, but a modality of existence that is identified as the problem. And considering that, at the advent of each economic crisis, vagabondage increased, everything must be done to capture or hide these escapees of the productive cycle. "There are aspects of evil that have such a power of contagion, such a force of scandal that any publicity multiplies them infinitely."[33] They are just beyond the immediate grasp of the apparatus, and always at risk of contaminating the productive process with the viral intensity of a different world and a different form-of-life. The ontological status of the astray is at stake in every instance of their activity. Those who go astray are always deemed to be on a warpath. "[B]etween the two worlds there can be only war, hatred, and fundamental hostility."[34]

However, one finds that even the fully employed exist in a shadow of an ever-present inward-facing delinquency. Through the eighteenth century, a shift took place regarding the various illegalisms the upper class could tolerate of the working population. As the emergent bourgeois class took control of the juridical and police apparatuses, the illegalisms of this new working class became the central target of repression and control. The prison, the army, the police: these all develop into means of breaking up lower-class illegalisms — some of which the bourgeois and feudal orders were party to. With these systems in place, theft, machine-breaking, rioting, and the formation of clandestine associations will all be targeted and fundamentally suppressed. With fraud and smuggling quelled and largely controlled, both by these forms of policing and new processes of production, a new need arises: the "need to set up an apparatus that is sufficiently discriminating and far-reaching to affect the very source of this illegalism: the worker's body, desire, need."[35] This illegalism deprives the owner not of his physical wealth, machines, buildings, or commodities. The dissipater "is someone that undermines, not capital, not riches, but his own labor-power." It is "no longer a bad way of managing one's capital, but a bad way of managing one's life, time, and body."[36] Dissipation is not an event, like the destruction of a machine, but a mode of existence. It is an ethos ultimately at odds with the espoused productivist morality of the disciplinary society. It is one that strays from the moral expectation and framework of labor itself. It is a relationship with oneself that deprives the factory owner of one's own labor-power. The dissipater is one who lives outside of the norm, which is an affront to the system of "ethical and political coercion that is necessary for the body, time, life, and men to be integrated, in the form of labor, in the interplay of productive forces."[37] The illegalist of dissipation is, at once, the enemy of both the capitalist owner of the means of production and the "sad militant" who can only identify the specter of revolution in the leveraging of labor-power.

This dissipation is a thread that can be traced through so many newly securitized apparatuses of production. Foucault himself saw it echoing among the Parisian youth of post-68. In a roundtable discussion, Paul Virilio — seemingly worried about the proletariat becoming "marginal" in the post-industrial world — asks, "what happens if this marginalization becomes a mass phenomenon? [...] In the nineteenth century it was a tiny segment of society; now let's admit that now these characteristics apply to millions of people in the suburbs." Foucault's response flips the premise of the question when he replies:

> What if it is the mass that marginalizes itself? That is, if it is precisely the proletariat and the young proletarians that refuse the ideology of the proletariat? [...] They are the young workers who say: why should I sweat my whole life for $2000 a month when I could... At that point, it's the mass that is becoming marginal.[38]

These are all modes of wandering outside the imposed regime of the norm. These are all methods of going astray, of entering into a zone of abnormality. It is for this reason that, throughout the eighteenth and nineteenth centuries, and possibly still today, the moral nomadism of the dissipator, whose mode of being is one perpetually in error, strikes such a unique fear.

Children fall through the stockades of the disciplinary apparatus and the circuitry of the biopolitical regime as well. In many ways, children are the most precious target of disciplinary and biopolitical management. A utopian socialist publication in nineteenth-century France retells an interaction between a judge and a boy charged with criminal vagrancy:

> "The judge: One must sleep at home. — Béasse: Have I got a home? — You live in perpetual vagabondage. — I work to earn my living. — What is your station in life? — My station: to begin with, I'm thirty-six at least; I don't work for anybody. I've worked for myself for a long time now. [...] I've plenty to do. — It would be better for you to be put into a good house as an apprentice and learn a trade. — Oh, a good house, an apprenticeship, it's too much trouble. And anyway the bourgeois ... always grumbling, no freedom. — Does not your father wish to reclaim you? — Haven't got no father. — And your mother? — No mother neither, no parents, no friends, free and independent." Hearing his sentence of two years in a reformatory, Béasse pulled an ugly face, then, recovering his good humor, remarked: "Two years, that's never more than twenty-four months. Let's be off, then!"[39]

His reaction seems rather strange, or comically absurd, especially in the face of the horror that is incarceration. However, here one ought to heed the words of Bataille: "When we laugh at childish absurdity, the laugh disguises the shame that we feel, seeing to what we reduce life."[40] This errant motion is not to be understood through the framework of basic transgression, however. No matter how helpful Bataille may be in this moment of reflection on the shame we carry as life becomes only the unfolding of its control, there is also a necessary break with such an understanding of childishness. To see transgression in the life of Béasse is to take the lens of legal authority; it is to peer into this life only by passing through the word of the law. For transgression remains entirely bound to law and to the doctrine of exclusion. The boy is asked for an account of himself, it is given, and immediately the punitive matrix works towards reintegration. The simple matrix of transgression and exclusion is inadequate here.

The moral nomadism that remains so thoroughly feared has to be understood through its centrifugal motion, and not simply a direct negation or a reversal of terms. Passing over to the other side of an apparatus that distinguishes between the "good boys" and the Béasses or the vagrant remains insufficient, and only serves to reproduce the assumptions that uphold the apparatus itself. Flipping the apparatus leaves it intact. Pushing beyond its boundary, in the name of transgression, only ensures that the boundary functions properly in its distinguishing of life that is proper or life that is astray, in error, and to be dealt with. Those who primarily approach the question of power critically through the frame of transgression "remain pegged to the general system of representation against which they were turned."[41] To stray is not to simply transgress. It is here where the figure of the pleb becomes the necessary compliment to the vagabond and a conception of straying. The measure of the pleb is a "counter-stroke"; it is "that which responds to every advance of power by a move of disengagement."[42] The plebian intensity is one of flight; it finds itself elsewhere. This disengagement is perhaps the most crystalized articulation of a destituent gesture in Foucault's corpus. To disengage from power is not the same as transgressing it. The motion of the pleb is, throughout history, a centrifugal one. This is why power is always reactive. When Foucault tells us resistance precedes power, we must take this assertion seriously. Power must always react to something it finds entirely enigmatic, because such threats expose the emptiness of its supposed relation to necessity.

The utopian managers of life who attest that we must strive towards an "optimization" of everything promise to deliver us a new world. Some of them even promise us entire new planets to lay waste to, like the crypto-accelerationist Nikolai Fedorov and his "common task" to "transform the solar system into a controlled economic entity."[43] Of course, this "common task" is hindered by "common drunkenness." The colonization of the stars must start at a colonization and total unification of every human body and its functions. Indeed, all techno-accelerationists demand this "multi-unity," where all are optimally thrown into a completely orchestrated world — a utopia of pure managed existence. They make this promise to deliver a new world, simply because they must foreclose on any other way to *live*. If only were we to not stray, they tell us, we could live *under* fully-automated luxury "communism." Of course, this is nothing other than an intensification of the operation of economy and the management of population. The illegalism of dissipation is the shared enemy of the cybernetician and the physiocrat and their respective "common" tasks. Whenever a utopian program is proposed, it is always penned with the promised blood of those it will seek out and deem suboptimal in the new "rational" organization of life. This is the common assurance voiced of the utopian techno-positivist: that freedom is found on the other side of optimization. But the optimization of life is, by design, an eliminative practice. Going astray is never optimal.

Through this errancy — that straying which the engineers and economizers of life ceaselessly work to render as an error to be corrected or erased — the undefined work of freedom comes into view.

LOST IN THE CIRCUITRY

There are those, on the other hand, who are embedded deep within a power relation, with very little space for evading ensnarement. So they press inward, getting lost in the subjectivating apparatus that is meant to tend towards reintegration. They expose the faulty orientation of the biopolitical circuitry and lean into it, causing it to either expose its own weaknesses and frailties, or to short-circuit altogether. With limited options and a subject-function imposed on them, they reverse the key conditions of the relation of power. For, in a very particular sense, they have a more intimate sense of the tools and technologies in play, even if they do not wield them. The refusal remains hidden within an affirmation of position that exposes the weakness of precisely what keeps them there.

For Foucault, the militant heroes of anti-psychiatry were not the likes of R.D. Laing, nor any practitioner. They were the hysterics pushing the epistemic security of psychiatric power to the point of collapse. The hysteric, as a clinical case, presented an immediate epistemological nightmare scenario for psychiatric power. "[T]he psychiatrist's knowledge is one of the components by which the disciplinary apparatus organizes the surplus-power of reality around madness."[44] The establishing of a domain of reality and the ascription of truth is completely in the hands of the psychiatrist on the floor of the asylum. The psychiatrist alone can thwart the crisis of madness and find its truth.

If, as Foucault suggests, psychiatrists acquired their role as defenders of the social against the aberrant dangers of the mad through their access to its reality, hysteria constitutes the worst kind of epistemological crisis. The hysteric in revolt is a figure that dissolves the veil of the psychiatrist's power, under the thin fabric that constitutes psychiatric power-knowledge lies everything the hysteric gave to the psychiatrist. Hysteria collapses the analytic walls between reality and simulation. It creates such a systematic shock to the functionality of psychiatric power that Jules Falret, whose work was foundational to initial theories of *folie à deux*, rational insanity, and mass behavioral phenomena as forms of social contagion, is left with no option other than to make one totalizing attestation: "The life of the hysterics is just a constant lie."[45] One is left comically wondering what such a desperate and carelessly diagnostic outburst means for Falret's several volumes of clinical study.

It is here where a critical intervention must be made. If we look to Falret's hysterics, it is not to hail them as some inherently emancipatory subject position; no such thing exists. This would also do a grave injustice to the struggle against carceral institutionalization. To do such a thing would be to take up a clinical gaze that is no different from the one that treats madness, mental illness, disability, and criminality as something pre-discursive and, importantly, naturalized. We aim instead to show the fragile reliance of psychiatric power on a particular produced subjectivity and the covalent bond between power and knowledge.

From the walls of the factory to the cell doors of the prison, one finds throughout this history of straying the identification of errant life as that which corrodes the properness of a given subject-function.

Moving to the twentieth century, in December of 1971, those incarcerated at the Toul prison revolted. Generally, the detainees would use methods of escape that the guards, wardens, and other officials knew how to respond to or counter: suicide or breakout. But this was not the strategy the prisoners at Toul utilized. Instead, a complete reorientation occurred. *A barricade arose within the walls of the detention center.* "They occupied it like one occupies a factory, a place of struggle."[46] The complex system of enclosure became their entrenchment. All the mechanisms that they had come to know so well through their cruel subjugation became tactical elements in their defense.

They took no hostages; they led the guards who had abused them to the gates of the now occupied prison and let them leave. In that moment, in this new territory behind the prison walls, the disciplinary objects of an uninterrupted regime of penality did away the entire practice of it. It was not simply an act of transgression, but of neutralization. Despite having chained prisoners to their beds for days on end, pushing prisoners frequently to suicide, and regularly administering sedatives against their will, the guards were let free.[47] The only place in France where the logic of political torture momentarily subsided was inside the Toul detention center, in the midst of a revolt. The prisoners chose to hold no leverage over the administrators beyond the building itself. Guards would be allowed back into their place of work only once they had recognized those they incarcerate "as a force with which one negotiates."[48] One can only imagine how insulting to the correctional bureaucrats of life it must have been to see their entire practice dispensed with. Foucault takes this revolt as proof that "we can call 'political' any struggle against established power when it constitutes a collective force, with its own organization, objectives and strategy."[49] A "collective force" is not to be understood as some circumscribed political constituency. Instead, it is a series of objectives and strategies that correspond to a particular mode of existence, one that — in the case of the Toul revolt — had been eternally absent from the discourse on penality: those who do not simply escape "their prison," but those who gesture to escape prison as such.

OUT FROM UNDER THE WHEELS

This journey through revolts within biopolitical circuitry will close in Denver, Colorado, in 1978. A disability advocacy group, ADAPT (then named "Atlantis"), had been campaigning for access to public transportation for over a year. Their requests went without response. This is a marginal population, on the margin of the productive apparatus, and therefore in the margins of the social order. Deprived of transportation, one can imagine the hubristic city officials not seeing much of a threat in this population they had so thoroughly restricted and confined. Later that year, the city of Denver's transportation department purchased a new fleet of buses — without lifts. The state of Colorado had imposed immobility on the disabled population of Denver. In the face of a complete monopolization of mobility, these protestors abandoned their respectable democratic predicates and opted for a quiet militancy that dispensed with any institutional intentions or invectives. Early on a Wednesday morning, thirty disabled militants barricaded an intersection and blocked two of these brand-new buses. Some even pulled their bodies under the chassis against the tires, preventing them from moving at all. There were attempts at arrest, but the increasing commotion and unexpected traffic made it nearly impossible. Of course, serendipitously, the police buses were not equipped with lifts either.[50]

Their imposed regime of immobility becomes the city of Denver's. They deployed the condition of their subject-function in such a way that, for a moment, it was generalized, and the individualizing power of the government of disability ephemerally dissipated. This act, this halting of a city, interrupted the flow of bodies, the flow of capital, and productive processes. The "concrete utopia of cybernetic Empire" was, at one node, for one moment, disrupted and disputed.[51] And though this militant act was focused, it scrambled busing, pulled police off their patrol routes, and stopped itinerant workers. To reduce this action to a simple reformist demonstration would be to completely misunderstand the present condition of biopolitical and ableist modernity. To be governed in biopolitical modernity is to circulate. As we have already discovered, disability is always interlinked with an ascribed ungovernability. To move through the circuitry of the cybernetic order is the definitive experience of governance in the metropolis, which is "not a city at all," but a "technical diagram drawn up to establish communication and establish control that spans the distance between heterogeneous elements."[52] Simply put, the biopolitical imperative to "make live" is to keep something in circulation. And, conversely, the thanatopolitical imperative to "let die" is to simply remove one from circulation. The Invisible Committee understands this better than any commentator or secondary scholar of Foucault:

> Once the division has been made between those to be supported and those to be allowed to die, it's not certain that those knowing they're destined for the human trash pile will still let themselves be governed.[53]

Every act that motions towards the insurrectionary, even if minor in its militancy, gestures at something beyond what is immediate to it. It gestures at another way to live by exposing the forces that separate life from what gives it form. To reduce these actions to an "infantile desire for immediacy" or a "pseudo-activity" is to simply yearn for the pastoral gaze and its diagnostic approach to life and its management. A political disposition that supplants the ethical for the pathological can only promise a program that separates and distinguishes life between the proper and improper, and such a critique does nothing but concede to the current disaster. It is actions like this that are not simply activities, but the exposing of a scandal of truth through errancy. This refined weaponization of the conditions of their subjugation disrupted an entire city and, for a moment, exposed the weakness of the circuitries that seamlessly subjugate all.

CONCLUSION: OTHER LIFE

Giorgio Agamben, calling upon the work of Walter Benjamin, remarks that "the state of exception turned into rule signals law's fulfilment and its becoming indistinguishable from life."[54] The law becoming indistinguishable from life — that is the horror at the core of the lingering state of exception that has defined modernity. One must say the same of the modern biopolitical apparatus: that its perfect functioning is found when life, its motions, habits, contingencies, and behaviors become indistinguishable from the processes of its policing and production. The terror of the norm reigns everywhere life and its policing enter a zone of indiscernibility. Biopolitical circuitry functions seamlessly when one can no longer identify its content or object as distinct from its management. The means of control become so vast, and so micropolitically precise, that one not only no longer notices them but begins to only give an account of themselves in accordance with them. One becomes a series of accreditations, failures, infractions, promotions, and positions. Deleuze describes the control society as comparable to a highway. "[B]y making highways, you multiply means of control," one can "travel infinitely and 'freely' without being confined while being perfectly controlled."[55] If one has to keep citing Deleuze on the highway as a political signpost, like what the anxious bureaucrats of political philosophy often reduce Marx to, it is because the crucial ethical import of his reflection on control is often actually lost. It becomes an almost purely aesthetic assertion. The control society, counter to what so many American and English pseudo-Deleuzian commentators like to attest, is *still fundamentally a punitive society*. To stray is to immediately, and criminally, enter into the bipolar dynamic of anarchy and abnormality. Beyond this, the refinement of these systems of biological security intertwines with the quiet intensification of a eugenic modernity that is coming to define the daily misery of bourgeois liberal democracies. One can travel freely while being perfectly controlled, so long as one is willing to be exposed to death in the name of the good governance of the population and the vitality of the social order.

The vignettes of a disabled teenager sleeping on hot asphalt under the shadow of a bus's wheel well, of a child grinning as he is taken to serve his sentence in a reformatory, or of a vagabond wandering in affirmation and search of a freedom industrialization has stolen from them — these are all images of errors in the flow-state that is the circulation of bodies, commodities, and debt that defines and confines everyday existence. They are those who have strayed from the norm and have failed to develop this circulative habit, and therefore present a danger. Some present a challenge to the disciplinary apparatuses that attempt to capture them and render them docile, others threaten the biopolitical salvation of the flock. However, they all are the presence of a different life, another life. They all manifest a truth that is deemed in its errancy absolutely intolerable. To become intolerable to what is absolutely intolerable in our present situation is to manifest a scandal of truth in the form of one's life. "Truth is an errancy, without which a certain person could not live."[56] In this sense, all of these straying lives share a resonance with one of the oldest insurgent philosophical forms of life: the cynic. As Foucault writes of the cynics in his final lectures: "There can only be true life as other life, and it is from the point of view of this other life that the usual life of ordinary people will be revealed as precisely other than the true."[57] The cynic attests to those horrified by their actions, that they in fact live in truth. This interplay between processes of subjectivation and the fluid dynamic of truth and error comes to constitute a central element in Foucault's work on normativity.

That this work on the cynic was Foucault's parting message to us is deeply important, and we ought to meditate on it in a meaningful way. When life becomes perfectly isomorphic with its systems of control, when it is consigned to and defined as the productive, when it never leaves the "highway," what kind of practice of freedom or desubjective self-refusal is possible? Nothing other than the production of the perfectly dividual citizen who is always exposed to death in the state of exception.

It is in errancy that one finds an affirmation of life. Abnormality, though it bears the etchings of a history of abuse, confinement, pathologization, castigation, and death, also carries a very particular and subversive freedom. It is a freedom of divergence; and it is this divergence that has always been, and will forever remain, undefined, nameless, and anarchic.

THE IMAGELESS IMAGE

REFUSAL UNTO DEATH

To affirm is not to bear, carry, or harness oneself to that which exists, but on the contrary to unburden, unharness, and set free that which lives.

Gilles Deleuze, "The Mystery of Ariadne
According to Nietzsche"[1]

When William of Paris and his coterie of inquisitors confronted fourteenth-century French mystic Marguerite Porete with charges of heresy, she evinced a disposition of unflagging obstinacy. Her manuscript *The Mirror of Simple Souls* recorded a controversial theology of the afterlife, a work inspired by Porete's own mystical experience. Steeled by divine insight, she refused to respond to the prodding interrogations of her accusers. Her reticence sparked their outrage, which ultimately led the Church to burn her at the stake. It is said that in her final moments of her brutal execution, Porete displayed utter equanimity. Her embodied faith moved the crowd of onlookers who met her calm gaze through the conflagration. Refusing to answer the tribunal, refusing to recant the ideas of her heretical manuscript, and refusing to show anguish as flames engulfed her body, Porete became a body of pure refusal. What germinated in her as a mystical vision and blossomed as a treatise on the beatific flight of the soul ultimately led Porete to extricate herself from the brutality of judgment. Porete's channeling of a divergent image of the divine, her contact with an untrammeled image of God Himself, manifested as a series of alterities: first as divine mystery, then as the heretical *The Mirror of Simple Souls*, and finally as a relentless otherness to order, which condemned her to death. The failure of the inquisitors to exact obedience and repentance casts Porete as the figure of refusal *par excellence*. Her acts of moral courage flowed from the affirmation of a God-image fundamentally at odds with the dogma espoused by her murderers. More than martyrdom, the silence threaded through her resistance unto death bound her to a *sacred conspiracy*.

Ordinarily, we would scarcely consider a brush with the divine in terms of its technicity. Porete's life nonetheless presents to us the possibility of a cybernetics of the epiphany, a quasi-functionalist view of mystical interventions in which divine revelation becomes a catalyst of a radical machinic singularity. Porete's life and death are not symbolic of refusal — they do not simply "stand in" for refusal as appearance thereof — they are an enactment of its very mechanism. Her reticence functions as a propaganda of the deed, and her act is inseparable from the force that propels this function into activity. Porete, moreover, does not merely leave behind a trace of fugitivity but rather throws open thresholds of escape and conspiratorial communication. The utter incommunicability of the incipient apocalypse is itself an image. Porete's embrace of the image bypasses the grid of intelligibility instituted by the dominant theology. Her legacy thus operates as an insurgent image destituting the dogmatic images propagated by the Church. Again, her refusal is not mere iconoclasm, but a complete slip of the Catholic Church's apparatus of capture, a withdrawal from its ocular registers.

Ultimately, what concerns us beyond Porete's case is a broader research of the function of images and the imagination itself in forms of political fugitivity. There is a persistent refrain within the discourse of emancipatory politics that urges us to envision a future capable of capturing our collective political imagination. Yet the current conjecture is packed in with a plethora of futures: from embryonic utopias awaiting the milk of human courage to the host of apocalyptic visions recycled unremittingly on popular streaming platforms. The truth is that our imagination has already been captured many times over — yet something remains lacking. In the end, only the worst of these futures can be realized, absent the efficient cause of an emancipatory will: a ferocious refusal of the present state of things.

The following treatment concerns refusal and imagination, the image of refusal, refusals of the imaginary, and images that refuse. Ours is not the disconsolate refusal of the pessimist but a spirited refusal of forces that assert power above life. Herein, we present a conceptual toolkit of tactical refusals for the subversion of images functionalized towards our domination. The refusal of particular images and specific concepts of the image are essential precursors to seeing through the seemingly spectral aspects of our political bondage. In our act of refusal, we find that the specters themselves are scintillations projected from a larger apparatus of capture, a machine parasitic upon the very same crystalline matrix of imagination from which our new futures speak.

Late-fifteenth or early-sixteenth-century French manuscript of The Mirror of Simple Souls. Unknown French copyist - Manuscript Chantilly, Musée Condé, F XIV 26, fol. 38 Marguerite Porete, The Mirror of Simple Souls, Chapter 35 (Dialogue of the Soul and Reason)

The prospects of our fugitivity also demand the flight of the images themselves. In other words, important to our own escape is the question of how an image itself is able to elude capture. How are we co-constituted with images within subjectivating apparatuses? What are the dominant images that suppress the images of autonomy and liberation? How can images thus function to frustrate or escape modes of capture? Lastly, how and where does the gesture of refusal appear amidst these other questions? Our inquiry demands the creation of a new concept we call "the imageless image."

THE IMAGELESS IMAGE

The imageless image begins with an act of philosophical refusal that shows a way out. It generates a set of thought-escape functions irreducible to a singular use. Every thought subsists in an "image" or an *image of thought*. This is to say our ideas are bound to presuppositions or that all philosophical paradigms maintain a presuppositional character. The concept of the imageless image itself is auto-evacuating, unable to be caught in a singular stable image of itself.

The imageless image also refers to a critical disposition towards what are conventionally understood as images. Here, the concept presents itself as a paradoxical formulation, which turns on an intentional equivocation: "an image without an image" refers to a treatment of images as fundamentally non-representational entities, fluid becomings that are forever "entifying" in ways that exceed representational schemata. Moreover, the imageless image refers to philosophical interventions made to unsettle all uncritical presuppositions, which inform the persistent ways we tend to imagine images and the nature of the imagination itself.

The imageless image also invokes a critical approach to our practical relationship with images as kinds of living entities irreducible to their meanings. Early psychoanalysis was notorious for enervating images of fantasy by rendering them into its constrained grids of intelligibility. Psychoanalysis and its imperialism of the image valorizes the utility of images to achieve specified outcomes whilst marginalizing their lively peculiarities. Our approach not only intends to rescue the image from reductive hermeneutics, but in doing so, present the image as a line of flight from various normalizing processes and subjectivating tendencies.

Furthermore, the imageless images implies a set of tactics of imperceptibility, methods of escaping the register of binary codes and making entities impervious to cybernetic capture. Our purpose is not to provide an exhaustive program of anti-ocular fugitivity but to highlight some important functions of the image in the politics of escape. For this, we reconsider Deleuze and Guattari's concepts of *creative involution*, *the crystal-image*, and *minor becomings* in conjunction with the nonrepresentational premises of the archetypal psychology advanced by James Hillman. This theoretical combination sparks a synergy intended to embolden the prospect of mobilizing *image work* as a material force for political liberation. Moreover, at the nexus of the work of these respective theorists, we widen the aperture of escape from the dogmatic image of thought infused by the deathly lure of Freud's Oedipus and fascistic *dividuality*. To be sure, our flight from psychoanalysis employs the very substance and insights of the discipline itself —

but as is often the case, the weapons we procure amidst the escape are found in the crawlspaces of the captor's lair. We appropriate their arsenals, invert their usages, and involute the structures that harbor their potencies. In short, the imageless image directly opposes the ocular or *dividual* image, whose epistemic grounds are formed by *the dogmatic image of thought*.

REFUSING THE DOGMATIC IMAGE OF THOUGHT

The imageless image first draws upon Deleuze's critique of *the image of thought*, or what he calls the *traditional* or *dogmatic image of thought*. Deleuze attempts to dismantle the dogmatic image of thought by executing an attack upon a set of dominant tendencies in Western philosophy: the act of engaging in theoretical labor whilst beginning with objective presuppositions or subjective presuppositions.[2] Objective presuppositions typically comprise a set of traditionally dominant philosophical beliefs with an unexamined basis. The principal objective presupposition in Deleuze's crosshairs is the view that thought is an activity inherently and necessarily tied to the notions of "the true" or "the good." Subjective presuppositions have also plagued philosophy with the conjecture that what is common or obvious is itself the appropriate starting point of thought. Deleuze indicates Descartes as a particular thinker who both successfully avoided and unfortunately succumbed to presuppositions in his own system of concepts. In formulating the concept of the *cogito*, as in the phrase "*cogito ergo sum*" ("I think therefore I am"), Descartes initially skirted a conceptual disaster, averting the claim that human beings were "rational animals." As Deleuze notes, Descartes avoided doing so as "the concept explicitly presupposes the definitions of these terms."

While he did not stumble by smuggling in objective presuppositions, Descartes failed to root out subjective presuppositions evident in his work. Subjective presuppositions express the conceit, "Oh that's obvious. That's something everyone knows" — the implication being that there exists something about the idea which doesn't merit the scrutiny we'd ordinarily apply to other ideas developed in a system of thought. This best applies to ideas lodged in the category of "common sense" (those ideas which embrace the fallacy that their widespread or familiar character automatically secures for them some sort of merit). The valorization of common sense as a first principle almost always begs the question of an argument's deeper epistemological justification. To eschew common sense as a philosophical starting point does not necessarily harm the pragmatics or indispensability of certain commonly held beliefs or values; what is problematic is the assertion that *a* common sense or something that *everyone* knows constitutes an unchallengeable entry point into philosophical inquiry.

Descartes' famous axiom "I think, therefore I am" furthermore suffers from other epistemological gaps. Deleuze observes that Descartes' claim presupposes the universality of concepts such as *thinking*, *being*, and *self*. Descartes not only presupposes these concepts as self-evident; he moreover fully commits to them as *natural* (a thought-terminating qualifier with a functional equivalence to common sense). By presupposing thinking, being, and self as universal concepts, the activity of thought merely instantiates categories prefigured under the Cartesian rubric. Under this rubric, individual instances of thought become reduced to diminished representations of the system's categories. In short, once you embrace the Cartesian presuppositions that *everybody* accepts, there is little thinking about thinking that can escape its loop of logic. Deleuze, however, assures us that we can extricate ourselves from the conceit of subjective presuppositions by simply refusing to be represented as one of the *everybody*. Just disallow others to speak on your behalf and demand that you are not part of the "Big Everybody"!

Deleuze's gesture of refusal in *Difference and Repetition* not only lies at the heart of challenging the dogmatic image of thought, as the spirit of refusal infuses the broader arc of concepts in his corpus. His reputation as a thinker of "pure positivity" may obscure this aspect of his work (namely in the subsequently explored concepts of *creative involution* and the *crystal-image*). The putative Nietzschean positivity of Deleuze has sparked some skepticism about the political strength of his work amidst what Badiou has called "the crisis of negation."[3] The challenge to combat the epochal impasse of an unabating capitalist realism, for instance, has fostered an impulse to reach for those philosophical concepts which embrace the negative or resound with a destructive tenor. The characterization of Deleuze as philosopher of the positive overlooks both the force and function he believes philosophy to maintain. He famously writes, "Philosophy does not serve the State or the Church, who have other concerns. It serves no established power. The use of philosophy is to sadden."[4] Deleuze's critical procedures function like a stent, opening wide and flushing out the narrows occluded by the conventional and the canonical. Thus, a kind of incipient violence is required to abolish "a 'rude fetishism' that tends to dichotomize our world into truths and appearances, causes and effects, subjects and objects."[5] As this fetishism continues to subsist deep in the circuitry of subjectivating forces, the activity of thought remains terminally confronted by a binarizing logic operative within the extant categories of experience. To subvert these tendencies demands that our thinking embody the spirit of refusal.

Ultimately, subverting the dogmatic image of thought returns thinking to the concrete potencies that instigate the movement of thought; in other words, the forces that lie outside of thought. For Deleuze, the incipient activity of thought is brought about involuntarily. It occurs in virtue of an "outside": a contingency of external forces which cause a rupture or an incitement to think. This involves being awakened from a kind of stupor or unconsciousness, which in turn instigates a search for truth. Deleuze's work in *Proust and Signs* explores the notion of the search and both its philosophical and non-philosophical dimensions.[6] Deleuze suggests that philosophy occurs as an "apprenticeship of signs," a search for truth that ascribes importance to non-philosophical endeavors as necessary to our philosophical journey. What we often erroneously construe as digressions from a philosophical life become, in fact, important moments of the philosophical apprenticeship. The apprenticeship, as Deleuze describes it, does not involve delimiting the field of philosophical inquiry as it does in Plato. Instead, it proceeds as "a literary apparatus that brings together heterogeneous elements and makes them function together; the work thus constitutes a whole, but this whole is itself a part that merely exists alongside the other parts, which it neither unifies nor totalizes."[7] Put another way, for Deleuze the search for truth involves the recovery of disparate moments of "lost time," which are then reconstructed in narrative fashion. A lifetime of wasted moments, romances that have come to pass, and time detracted from artistic or aspirational projects converge in the revelation that such events were elements of a philosophical project — but one irreducible to a totalizing unity as such. Thus, becoming philosophical involves a recovery of time that we consummate through the activity of creating sense. The creation of a new sense involves formulating a linkage of disparate experiences. This connection does not occur in virtue of a presupposed unity, but rather in the specifying of differential processes, which trace a non-organic and transversal line through our experience. Ultimately, an important ethical task of philosophical life we uphold is cultivating a congruence with the heterogenous and multiple character of our existence.

THE FUGITIVITY OF CREATIVE INVOLUTION

The function and significance of the concept of *involution* transforms throughout the corpus of Deleuze's writing. The term "involution" can refer to a spectrum of processes characterized by their refusal or deactivation of organizing axioms. The imageless image also refers to the involution of epistemologies and hermeneutical frameworks, which function to terminally resituate images back into a symbolic order that denies them their particular eventfulness and autonomy.

At base, involution refers to a process of *enfolding*

in contradistinction to *evolution*, which is generally typified by the act of *unfolding*.[8] The concept of evolution, as we understand it, is pegged to the notions of progress and regress. Evolution implies an axial schematic of ideal poles by which either progress or regress can be measured. Involution, on the other hand, refers to an act of enfolding that occurs in the absence, collapse, or evacuation of such binarizing logic. The evolutionary binary privileges a scalar movement along designated axes, whereas the involutionary movement "involves" forces excluded from polar configurations along a series of transversal axes.

We can also understand involution in its common negativized medical denotation: the shrinkage or atrophy of an organ in the body due to its inactivity. The shrinkage entails the folding inward of the organ upon itself. What's more, when an organ atrophies, it might be the case that surrounding organs envelop the space produced by the shrinkage. In a creative involution, however, the organ that is deactivated is specifically that which organizes other organs and gives them their "organ-ized" character. The organized character of an organ is its characteristic function. Such a function is marked by its integration into a system of inputs and outputs that simultaneously delimits the variety of possible activity. Hence, the creative involution of an organized array of components entails a rupture or refusal of its organizing principle. To be sure, creative involution is not a regression in the manner in which we might consider the failure of a bodily organ; to regress means to become less differentiated or less "involved" with the particular potencies that constitute the event of differentiation.[9] The involutionary act thus frees the parts, processes, and potencies from their polarized series or organized assemblages to either function in relative autonomy or enter into new assemblages. Creative involution is not what we might call "escape-in-itself" but it nevertheless effectuates a tactically necessary withdrawal from an apparatus of capture.

Deleuze puts forward the "the involuted body" of the anorexic to illustrate the dynamics of a creative involution. The prime objective of the involuted body is locating a sustainable line of flight from the intersubjective tensions that strive to regiment it through processes of normalizing power. Deleuze by no means intends to romanticize the plight of the anorexic; rather, he bypasses a familiar pathological judgment of symptoms to highlight the functionalism of the anorexic body as a body of refusal, one which invents micropolitical strategies of evasion from patriarchal domination and capitalist exploitation.

In his conversations with Claire Parnet in *Dialogues II*, Deleuze pays tribute to his wife, Fanny, whose own struggle with anorexia he centers as a model of escape and subversion. He observes that the anorexic body is an *anorganic* body tilted in opposition against the organ-izing logic of its world. "It is not a matter of the refusal of the body, it is a matter of a refusal of the organism, of a refusal of what the organism makes the body undergo."[10] The anorexic body engages in acts of rebellion, subverting the rituals of patriarchy and consumer society imposed upon it by cultivating a battery of counter-habits, interruptions, and obfuscations. A sufferer of anorexia may adopt their own rituals, such as going back and forth between the table, the kitchen, and other areas of a home to disrupt the rhythms of the sedentary mealtime ritual. Deleuze also notes that it is often the case that anorexics become models (to seize the means of representing the body image) or cooks (to seize the means of food preparation). An anorexic may also become "a peripatetic cook," often acting as the preparer of meals in different social groups to avoid having to sit down to eat.[11]

However, in their avoidance of food, the anorexic individual must make certain concessions. The inevitable pangs of hunger call them back to the consumerist and patriarchal regimes. One must find sustenance amidst the act of refusal, but not without mitigating certain risks. By reimagining the constitution of food itself, the anorexic body is able to strengthen its resistance towards the impulse to eat. Deleuze writes that anorexics imagine food being filled with "grubs and poisons, worms and bacteria," inducing them to spit out bites of food not yet swallowed. The anorexic "wrests particles from food," absorbing a modicum of nutrients. Their refrain: "Trick-the-hunger, trick-the-family, trick-the-food."[12] This multiplicity of strategies plays a part in preventing the anorexic person from being absorbed back into a milieu dominated by the fantasy of patriarchal values.

What we might ordinarily call an anorexic individual's "symptoms" take part in an intense technical regulation of the body's inputs and outputs to create a kind of non-locatability on the social register. Given the importance of the image and the imaginary as operators in the fugitivity of the anorexic body, we are forced to confront some more general questions about the role of the imagination and its technicity in acts of refusal: what other "symptoms" expressed amidst our impulses, dreams, and fantasies also echo the yearning of would-be fugitive-machines? Could this machine ever be assembled adequately within anything resembling a psychotherapeutic context? What would be the conditions for the possibility of a thriving fugitive-machine?

THE CRYSTAL-IMAGE VERSUS THE THEATRICS OF THE IMAGINARY

For us, the idea that images both arise from and fall back upon an immanent sphere of social production is non-controversial. Instead, we must question the specific ontological status of the image and the prospects that a new hermeneutics of the image presents for fugitivity. Again, we turn to Deleuze to interrogate the presuppositions that commonly undergird notions of image and the imagination. The ontology of the image and our ethical regard for it stem from an epistemological basis bound up in the dogmatic image of thought, which, of course, Deleuze refuses.

In the interview entitled "Doubts About the Imaginary," Deleuze advances his skepticism towards the ontological status of the term "imaginary." The imaginary, in its many traditional formulations, most often refers to the domain of the imagination as an interiorized generative locus of images.[13] However, Deleuze's avoidance of the imaginary as a positive concept does not preclude the idea that images themselves are potentially transformative; rather, Deleuze refuses the notion of the imaginary to cast into sharper relief the more extensive ontological apparatus from which images are produced. The matter does not seem entirely settled for Deleuze, as his treatment of the imaginary in the interview remains haunted by some of the ambivalences that motivate our work here. In any event, he nonetheless insists on deposing the imaginary through a sweeping epistemological reformulation that elevates *the powers of the false*, a concept which asserts the generative powers of falsity largely suppressed by the notion of truth as it has been most commonly understood throughout the history of Western epistemology.

Among Deleuze's analytic of concepts, it is the tension that exists between *the concept of the true* and *the concept of time* that pre-empts a traditional concept of the imaginary gaining a foothold in his philosophy.[14] Deleuze follows Bergson in establishing his concept of truth by asserting that *the real* and *the true* have been often badly conflated. Deleuze instead articulates a different set of distinctions to challenge the primacy of the conventional logic of the true-false/real-unreal axes. The propositions of Deleuze's reformulation are as follows: the real opposes the unreal (the imaginary), truth opposes falsity. Ordinarily, truth manifests in the conjunction of the real and the true, thus making true propositions accord with real states of affairs and allowing truth to be *representable* as such. The imaginary on its own is not false; it is only largely because of the accepted exclusive conjunction of the real and the true that the conjunction of the real and the false has been rejected. Given that the traditional model lacks unchallengeable grounds to establish itself in absolute terms, the distinctions Deleuze elaborated leave open a way of conceptualizing the false independent of the representational protocols of truth. What ultimately distinguishes the true from the false is that "only the true has a form (*eidos*); the false has no form, and error consists in giving the false the form of the true." The form of the true thus derives from the power of *judgment*. Judgment functions in virtue of presupposing the validity of the real in conjunction with its putatively unflagging capacity to instantiate "true" propositional content. Moreover, the form of the true itself manifests ultimately by its own conceit, whereby it serves to propagate an undisputed reception of its alleged necessity and universality. In other words, the form of the true is not established by an *a priori universality of fact*, i.e., by a self-validating principle that begs the question of how truth on its own evinces the power to undergird fact. Rather, the thought that conceives the true establishes truth by *the universality of right*, a force that presupposes the true and its form outside of the terms of its internal logic. The force in question is the inherently creative character of thought itself.

For Deleuze, what ultimately puts the concept of truth in crisis is the concept of time. The concept of the true contends with the concept of time in their shared stature as universals. Conventionally, what can be deemed true (or not true) can change in accord with the arrow of linear time; however, this fact alone does nothing to unsettle truth's hold on its claim to universality. It is time *itself*, time as a becoming, or what Deleuze calls "pure time," which frees the false from the duress of truth.[15] A certain traditional concept of the imaginary ultimately remains bound to signification and thus subordinate to a concept of truth, but in the "presentation of pure time," the form of time itself, a rupture of contingent temporal relations becomes possible via the powers of the false. Pure time subverts the despotism of the form of the true in the affirmation of time's ability to construct singularities unbounded by *a priori* and *formed* conceptions of universality.

Deleuze ascribes a generative power to falsity, a

becoming, which notably finds expression within stylistic forms of cinema that play with time in nonorganic or non-chronological ways. Doubtless, invoking the powers of the false involve acts we ordinarily construe as "imagining." However, for Deleuze, the phenomenality of the imagined does not reduce to or condense upon a notion of the imaginary as such. He avoids recourse to a hypostatization of the imagination as it tends to smuggle thought back into the constraints of representational thinking. Deleuze, however, presents an alternative: "To imagine is to construct a *crystal-image*, to make the image behave like a crystal."[16] The concept of the crystal-image involutes the structure of time, compressing the past and present into an admixture of the actual and the virtual, the real and the imaginary. For Deleuze, the concept of a crystal-image eludes the familiar entanglements of the unreality of the conventional imaginary as well as the imperious demands of the true. He sees the crystal-image as a font of becomings, a "circuit of exchanges."[17] In the crystal-image, linear temporality and its regime of judgment are dissolved. The coalescence of truth and falsity in the crystal-image causes it to scintillate, activating the powers of the false, those primordial forces that form the conditions for the possibility of creating the new.

What's more, the powers of the false return to us those putatively negative embodiments of the soul disparaged by Aristotle.[18] In the Aristotelian conception, only those images that conform to the model of the true are worthy of modifying our bodies and minds. Thus, the invention of "the true" as its own fantasy has involved repressing or psychically denying aspects of ourselves deemed unworthy of embodiment. These repressions may then manifest in dreams and fantasies as various menageries of monstrosities, guilds of tricksters and beguilers, and other legions of phantasmic beings. These entities engender various libidinal valences, manifesting themselves in the form of different images to become the *prima materia* of psychoanalysis and other forms of image work. As we will see, psychoanalytic hermeneutics has struggled to extricate itself from its own bondage within a traditional image of thought. However, a series of successive critical operations within and beyond the discipline psychoanalysis have afforded us leverage on the possibility of a new politics of the image.

IN PRAISE OF SURFACES

> *In the dream, mankind, in epochs of crude primitive civilization, thought they were introduced to a second, substantial world: here we have the source of all metaphysic. Without the dream, men would never have been incited to an analysis of the world.*
> Friedrich Nietzsche, *Human, All Too Human*[19]

Deleuze's disdain of dreams is not a refusal of dream images themselves. Rather, he directs his animus towards those intent upon dispossessing dreamers and dream images alike of a creative potency that lies beyond mere interpretation of an image. "Groups that are deeply interested in dreams, like psychoanalysts or surrealists, are also quick to form tribunals that judge and punish in reality: a disgusting mania, frequent in dreamers."[20] Following the criticisms of Antonin Artaud, Deleuze insists that certain hermeneutical strategies only threaten images with vivisections. He urges us to leave dreams behind for a "new dream," one whereby "the dream has taken the real movement upon itself," one which engenders sleeplessness, insomnia, and intoxication.[21] *The somnambulant nomad over the recumbent analysand*. We can imagine a dreamer of the new dream and their relationship to the image as analogous to the meandering of the nomad: a continuous flux marked by aleatory disclosures, disruptions, and surprises. The dreamer of the new dream bounds over the black holes of subjectivation, both the Oedipal depths and typological reductions propounded by the psychoanalyst. The image of the new dream is typified by its continuous surface — this is not the absence of depth per se, but the affirmation of depth as comprised of enfolded surfaces. A better question: What movements, migrations, or becomings can an image induce in the absence of a prefigured depth? Deleuze ultimately abandoned the problem of surface-depth in favor of the concept of *the body without organs*.[22] But perhaps taking up an older line of criticism in his work is in order, as nothing continues to plague the various lineages of psychoanalysis than the notion of depth! Transcending the metaphor of depth functions to unsettle the opposition that psychoanalysis formulates between putative nodes of repression or blockages and the existence of a "latent content" within the unconscious. We do not deny the existence of the libidinal forces said to exist in the depths; rather, we affirm their multiplicity, mutability, and modularity as constituted on a surface or series of surfaces. In other words, we elevate the importance of problematizing depth as "profound surfaces" that occlude their composition in the passional delirium produced by subjectivation. To see surfaces within depths is a precondition for escape. Guattari, in an episode of his own self-analysis of a dream, writes:

It is possible to use a model in which the unconscious is open to the future and able to integrate any heterogenous, semiotic components that may interfere. Then, meaningful distortions no longer arise from an interpretation of underlying contents. Instead, they become part of a machinist set up entirely on the text's surface. Rather than be mutilated by symbolic castration, recurring incomplete goals act instead as autonomous purveyors of subjectivation. The rupture, the breach of meaning, is nothing else than the manifestation of subjectivation in its earliest stage. It is the necessary and adequate fractalization which enables something to appear where the access before was blocked. It is the deterritorializing opening.[23]

The question remains how to preserve the phantasmagoric flows from the breach, how to let an image live and "entify" before the semantic membrane forecloses upon the rupture.

Now in our retort are the concepts of the crystal-image and a radical notion of surface. Together, they effectuate an alchemy of the imageless image, which lays bare black holes and potential paths of escape. The imageless image eschews "in-oculation" and depends rather upon enucleation, the removal of the introjected symbolic eyes, such as the figure of Oedipus. In-oculations occur on those surfaces riddled with depths, black holes. In-oculations are also those injections of symbolic eyes into the image: prefigured meanings or interpretations that suppress an image's lines of flight. Freud's analysands became inured to the incessant in-oculations of the Oedipal narrative. His method of analysis was a massive feedforward apparatus designed to overcode the production of fantasies with the image of the family. The figure of the family became a clearinghouse for every impulse, ceaselessly conditioning the analysand's internal monologue to engage in oedipalized auto-confession. The vacuous character of imageless image diffuses the gravitational pull of the Oedipal event-horizon. The rupture at once provokes a fractalization of the image and collapses the imperium of the repressive Oedipal symbology in an act of creative involution.

DIVIDUALITY AND THE *DIVIDUAL IMAGE*

François Laruelle has claimed that philosophy is the capital-form of thought — we contend that *psychoanalysis is the capital-form of the image*.[24] Psychoanalysis involves a series of operations that extract a surplus from the accounts of dreams, images, and fantasies in a way that often betrays the singularity of an image or fantasy. This betrayal is the reduction of the dream, image, or fantasy to the psychic labor of producing the surplus which is interpreted by the analyst. The analysand, upon entering analysis, acquiesces to a regime of signification, upon which a therapeutic process depends. To be analyzed is to risk subjecting a lively fantasy to the circularity of interminable reference. As there is seemingly no end to the ongoing expropriation of psychic labor power, that there is always more to interpret, one is never done with therapy. There is always posited an unexploited resource, an undiscovered frontier, a pristine content that threatens to elude the promulgation of psychoanalytic logic. In other words, the signs themselves serve to solicit a form of indenture that ensures regular transactions of images for interpretations. The utter impossibility of psychoanalysis abandoning the dictates of its regime of signification is analogous to capitalism's undying hunger for new frontiers of exploitation. Capitalism's incessant demand for surplus essentially forbids the possibility of capital overcoming the ever-shifting crosshairs of indifference and hostility, which it trains on various forms of life. Similarly, constantly valorizing an image's meaning over its event terminally pre-empts our relationality with the image as a form of life.

The more general problem we observe is that the fantasy becomes divested from its potency when rendered into *any* reductive interpretation. We are thus pressed to find a hermeneutical operation that does not assert a set of truth conditions that inevitably foreclose upon the image in its lively falsity. Here again, we refer to Deleuze's criticisms of the imaginary: when confronted with the form of the true, the image risks a negation of its constitutive forces. As a representation, the image is essentially forced to say "no" to aspects of its own eventfulness. That said, we should be careful to delineate between interpretation as representation from different therapeutic modalities developed over the various lineages of psychoanalytic disciplines. Some of these modalities do not directly depend upon uncovering the alleged "truth" of the image. Free association, active imagination, and other kinds of image work serve to tease out or enliven aspects of fantasy without necessarily explicating its meaning. The practice of active imagination in particular involves instigating aleatory dialogues with imagined figures in a manner independent of truth as such. Such modalities are forms of fabulation, which directly invoke the powers of the false proper to Deleuze's crystal-image. The challenge of preserving the image thus in part lies in cultivating a treatment or care of the image, which does not wholly depend upon making recourse to a hermeneutics of veracity. To be clear, we are not dismissive of therapeutic possibilities in our relationship with images; we only note that traditional psychotherapeutic schemata have tended towards sacrificing our capacity to relate to images in a non-appropriative manner.

As the capital-form of the image, psychoanalysis is a veritable *mise en abyme* ("the story within the story") of the broader sphere of social subjection. The image has become its own subject of operativity, turning images into *dividualities*. An image or fantasy becomes a dividuality through an interpretive intervention, which merely reduces an image to *what it represents or stands-in for*. Such an operation effectively renders it into a series of correspondences or references to be measured, translated, and indexed according to *ocular* schemata.

The term "dividuality" comes from the Latin term *dividuum*, whose earliest uses are found in the Roman comedies of Plautus and Terence. In the comedies, the term refers to a patriarchal system of property division. *Dividuom facere* designates a practice of Ancient Rome's ruling class, which involved the parsing and allocation of surpluses generated by sex workers and slaves. The practice entailed a calculus whereby human assets would be divided, and the wealth generated by these subordinates would be distributed among owners laying claim to various strands of surplus. This mechanism of appropriation pre-empted claims of the workers themselves to the spoils of their own labor. Thus already baked into this early concept of dividuality is a notion of primary accumulation analogous to pre-capitalist exploitation.[25]

The term *dividuum* is later picked up by Nietzsche to describe the introjection of pastoral power by individuals, or rather, *dividuals*.[26] For Nietzsche, a dividual is someone whose hatred of life masquerades as a project to achieve moral absolution in acts of "selfless sacrifice." The dividual desires to negate the multiplicity of drives encompassed by our "in-dividuality." In what is ultimately a bargain with death, the dividual risks a totalizing libidinal investment in a fragmentary or "dividualized" desire. Their lives are characterized by an ethical urgency which attempts to flee the multifarious and often contradictory compulsions of being an individual. The dividual clings to an immersive wish, drive, or longing, driven by a yearning for an all-consuming self-abnegation. Nietzsche presents to us a handful of figures inclined towards such pretensions: the devout lover, the doting mother, and the impassioned patriot.[27]

The first volume of Klaus Theweleit's extensive study of the fascist delirium, *Male Fantasies*, puts forward the most extreme cases of dividuality in the Nietzschean sense of the term.[28] The fascist as protector of faith and fatherland becomes enveloped by his infatuations of being mutilated on the battlefield. He indulges a meditation on death as an event of selfless dissolution where all are drowned in the blood of battle — comrades and enemies alike. He dreams of losing himself in an act of sacrifice on the battlefield, propitiating those gods who would rid the world of its moral degeneracy.

The fascist dividual divides themselves insofar as they detach their will and conscientious activity from their body and its various potencies for action. The fascist body is a cog, a tool, a divided component made up of other regimented components. The fascist may be a killing-machine, plugged into a rifle, with his arms forming a reloading-firing mechanism under the direction of the head and eyes. Yet the fascist fantastically and falsely alienates his will. His directing and piloting force is displaced fantastically onto the figure of the Führer, whose etymological root is leading and piloting. The fascist gives themselves up to the ecstasy of the Führer's enjoyment, and in this way becomes cybernated, automated, their body a pure vehicle for power with its internal principle elsewhere. Hitlerian waves stream across the fascist's body; they baptize the meat in discipline and confirm it in control. Moreover, fascist dividuality remains assiduously regulated by abstemious practices of libidinal retention. The fascist refuses pleasures only to make a hecatomb of his desire in the hatred and attrition of war. He thus fears pleasure as the dissipation of his illusory totality, his Being of beings. The fascist abhors premature expenditures of desire, which sap the intensities of their hermetically secured fantasy. In the figure of the fascist, we observe the extent to which the abasement of myriad drives can mobilize itself as a force for suppression and annihilation.

In the latter part of his life, Deleuze takes the concept of the dividual further, employing it to describe the breakdown of the individual into a fragmented ontology of cybernetic indexes, data points, and partial identities in his analysis of the societies of control. What we now call metadata comprises a large portion of our dividual profile: an aggregate of browser histories, online purchases, social media activity, etc., which coalesces into a user's cybernetic silhouette. For Deleuze, dividuality is characteristic of the *control society* (as distinct from the concept of Foucault's *disciplinary society*) in which the paradigm of social control tends towards mobilizing flows of data to expand surveillance, motivate consumer habits, and optimize apparatuses geared towards generating forms of compliance. The image of a control society is one in which access to delimited partitions of a controlled grid (a city district, a virtual space, etc.) remains tethered to variances or intervals of dividualized data flows. It is the image of William Gibson's Sprawl, *Blade Runner*'s Los Angeles, but it is systemically isomorphic with everything from apartheid border regimes to cashless urban transit systems.

The previous conceptual renderings of dividuality present various components from which we can assemble a concept of a *dividuated image*. First and foremost, a dividuated image is a coded image, one fatally subordinated to a representational schema. This aspect of the concept addresses the most encompassing challenge of the imageless image, which is to spare the image from a familiar hermeneutical knife. When images are coded with meanings, they become objects of correspondence or imitation, losing their immediacy and vitality. Under the rubric of meaning, some intensities pass and others do not. Those who might posit that an image maintains multiple meanings merely exacerbate the problem we intend to overcome. This pluralistic approach simply distributes the surplus value of images along an increased quantity of representational vectors in a manner similar to *dividuom facere*. Additionally, a dividuated image is an image to which we have precluded our own involvement as those enacting its fantasy. In sacrificing the image to representation, we also sacrifice our intimate relationality to the image.

At this juncture, we must introduce an important premise advanced by Hillman: that we are primarily composed of agonies, not polarities.[29] Hillman writes that our Dionysian consciousness experiences its conflicts in the form of dramatic tensions in which we are mutually situated within a given fantasy as *dramatis personae*. For Hillman, fantasies are performances in which we don masks amidst encounters with other masks.[30] The enactment of a fantasy remains irreducible to a separation and analysis of its elements. In other words, we cannot preserve the intensities or becomings of images without our own intimate and performative involvement with them. Hillman asserts the positive character of this encounter against a faulty *conceptual* understanding of fantasies. We abandon an intimate relationality to images when they are understood merely in terms of a set of characteristics or degrees of tensions along an axis of opposing poles, i.e., the categorical oppositions found in the traditional Jungian framework of light/dark, masculine/feminine, and so on. While Deleuze would likely balk at the theatrical or mimetic connotations invoked by Hillman, he might nonetheless agree that his treatment of the image privileges a manner of differencing irreducible to putative categories of experience. Lastly, the dividuated image evokes the property relation operative in *dividuom facere*. For example, a representational view of the dreams and fantasies typically involves a semantic rendering of their content onto an attributive schema. The involution of the dividual image entails a deeper intimacy or relationality with the fantasy. To move ahead in enlivening this relationality, we continue the work of unsettling the presuppositional foundations of psychoanalysis, namely the discipline's persistent fetishization of a monism that sacrifices pluralism.

EXIT THROUGH THE OSSUARY

In the plateau "One or Several Wolves?," Deleuze and Guattari turn to Freud's analytic relationship with "the Wolf-Man" as a sort of paradigmatic negative model of Freud's Oedipal monism. The multiplicities of creatures that frequently appear in the Wolf-Man's dreams and fantasies offer an apt starting point from which we can begin to trace a particular evolution of psychoanalysis away from its monistic tendencies and towards a more favorable treatment of multiplicity. The question of multiplicity does not simply concern the nature of images themselves, it also provokes a further interrogation of the presuppositions that ground the goals of the discipline itself, namely the notion of Freud's "cure" and the process of individuation espoused by Jung. We strive to dismantle the monistic predilection of psychoanalysis and how it has fabricated an impasse to the fugitivity of the image.

Sergei Pankejeff, whom Freud dubbed "the Wolf Man," was born into an aristocratic Ukrainian family. He struggled to meet the expectations of his station in life whilst suffering from childhood illnesses and neurotic episodes. Throughout his analysis with Freud, a relationship that spanned decades, Pankejeff not only presented Freud with troubling memories of his youth but also shared with him fantasies marked by a diverse menagerie of animals. Throughout his life, he experienced various animal-related phobias, developing fears of bugs and wolves. Pankejeff also mentions throughout his treatment that, as a young boy, he had a penchant for mutilating caterpillars and tormenting other insects and animals.

Freud believed the insects crushed by Pankejeff represented little children analogous with the figure of the forlorn child of Pankejeff himself. Despite the multiple bugs that perished in Pankejeff's own pincers, ultimately it is only ever *a singular* child who gets crushed in the Freudian reduction. Freud's tendency to impose familial personae upon images is commonly known, however; the analysis of Pankejeff serves to highlight Freud's curious animus toward the presence of the multiple. He expresses this prejudice most prominently when interpreting a childhood dream Pankejeff often recalls in the course of their sessions, the dream from which "the Wolf Man" earned his namesake. The dream begins with a young Pankejeff lying in his bed. He is startled by the sudden opening of the bedroom window. Peering through the window, the boy catches sight of six or seven white wolves perched among the branches of a nearby walnut tree. The wolves' tails seemed to have been replaced by bushy fox tails, each varying in color (another articulation of multiples). With claws out and ears pricked, the wolves' menacing glares terrify the young Pankejeff, who believes he's about to be devoured.

Once Freud corrals the wolves of the dream into his own bestiary — one conspicuously absent of animals — they are separated from their packs. Each become reduced to an Oedipal child transmogrified by the threat of castration. An inverted lycanthropy, perhaps. Rather than sticking to the images of Pankejeff's dreams and navigating their affective contours, Freud avoids maintaining the specificity of the account, always finding his way back to the Oedipal triangle.

In "One or Several Wolves?," Deleuze and Guattari also recall an infamous exchange between Jung and Freud, in which Jung conveys a significant dream to his mentor. In the dream, Jung finds himself exploring a richly furnished two-story house he identifies as his home. Descending into its deepest subterranean corridors, he ultimately discovers two shattered skulls, other broken bones, and some pottery fragments strewn about the dusty floor. Jung recounts the frustration he felt upon Freud's reaction to the dream:

> What chiefly interested Freud in this dream were the two skulls. He returned to them repeatedly, and urged me to fund a wish in connection with them. What did I think about these skulls? And whose were they? I knew perfectly well, of course, what he was driving at: that secret death wishes were concealed in the dream. [...] I felt violent resistance to any such interpretation.[31]

Jung remarks that Freud was also taken aback by the appearance of multiple skulls in the dream rather than there being just one. "A bone or a skull is never alone," write Deleuze and Guattari. "Bones are a multiplicity."[32] Bones connect to bones; they form a distribution of conjoined components. Finding a single bone often sparks a mystery, prompting a search for the other bones and a related set of artifacts. The imaginary-as-ossuary is itself jointed too, rich with a multiplicity of skeletal imagery, bone idioms, and other associations: we have bones to pick, criticisms that cut close to the bone, skeletons in the closet, and not to mention our own personal catacombs of haunted memories.

Freud's response forecloses upon the multiplicity immediately present in the bone-filled midden, disregarding *what saliently appears* to Jung, the dreamer. What's more, Freud advances the speculation that an unconscious desire for death lurks within the presupposed unity of Jung's fantasy. Freud suppresses the presentation of an image as an array or montage and instead enshrouds a fragment of the dream image (a single skull), smothering it with a totalizing interpretation, stifling the image as it was fantasized. With the Oedipal singularity fully superimposed upon the image of the skull (and with alleged death drives lurking about), we might catch the scent of Nietzsche's dividual in the offing. In any event, the multiple was suppressed.

THE COMPOSITION OF THE UNCONSCIOUS IN JUNG AND DELEUZE

When Jung scoured the detritus in the cave, he uncovered an image that arguably helped leverage his split with Freud, perhaps pushing him further towards his own theory of *archetypes*. Jung presents archetypes as figural embodiments of what he termed the *complexes of the psyche*. For Jung, each one of us lives in relation to a veritable pantheon of gods, heroes, and monstrosities whose modern imaginal manifestations take the form of a host of psychological dispositions. For Jung, the substrate of archetypal energies comprises an oppositional flux typified by a series of binary poles with shifting intensities (masculine/feminine, light/dark, ego/

shadow, etc.). The unconscious constellations of these oppositional tensions push and pull at us in their bid to become conscious. Jung calls the bringing of unconscious forces into the light of consciousness *individuation*, a process by which *the self* attains its realization. Individuation entails the integration of disparate archetypal figures, ultimately allowing one to transcend the agon of oppositional forces from which they emerge.

Jung believed that the journey of individuation first begins in an encounter with the *anima* or *animus*: our own personalized figures of the unconscious itself. In Jung's formulation, the anima/animus typically expresses itself in the form of a personage of the opposing gender. The appearance and affective contours of these figures tend to evolve as the process of individuation progresses. For Jung, becoming individuated is predicated upon successful integrations of our *shadow*. The shadow is expressed in imaginal projections of our negativity or that which we see as "other" to ourselves. It presents itself in opposition to the *ego*, the aspect of ourselves that constructs and regulates the boundary between an inside and outside. The ego not only mediates external social pressures but also those emergent desires of our unconscious life. The tension of oppositions produced at the nexus of the ego/shadow binary comprises the very substance of the individuation process. Clinically speaking, the resolution of these tensions can be a complicated and prolonged affair; however, Jung famously suggests that "[w]e don't so much solve our problems as we outgrow them."[33] What Jung refers to as integration is thus not a simple negation of affective negativity, but an unlocking of libidinal potencies trapped within the complex itself. "Growth" for Jung thus involves the holistic incorporation of the separated potencies which make us who we are *in toto*.

For Jung, the formative events of the individuation process tend to express a broadly polytheistic comportment, but the process culminates in a manner that is firmly monotheistic, if not ultimately Christian in character. Jung notes that our early brushes with the unconscious tend towards expressions of pagan mythologems or motifs. These images often express a partiality or incompleteness uncharacteristic of the symbols of monotheistic integration. The incipient fantasies of the individuation process might involve gods or creatures with a specific magical power but who also engender curious humanlike affects and peculiar shortcomings. These could be archetypal iterations of Hades, Hercules, or Persephone — or one might encounter various coyotes, ravens, or nymphs found in indigenous folklores. Regardless, the images of Jung's unconscious present themselves in the service of a prospective individuation. As the process of individuation progresses, new symbols of the self tend to appear to us: mandalic shapes, Christ-like entities, or other unitary figures signal the progressive integration of the once disparate aspects of the self. In Jung's view, our paths to individuation are different at the symbolic level because the constitution of individuals is different; however, the arc of progress nonetheless tends toward diminishing the multiplicity characteristic of the anima/animus stage. Jung viewed this generalized activity of the unconscious as a precursor in the same way that polytheism is sometimes imagined as a historical pre-stage to the rise of monotheisms.

Despite Deleuze's general allergy to religious

sentiment, he regards Jung's theory of archetypes as a step towards extricating the unconscious from Oedipal dogma. Thus it is vital to see the role of Jung as a figure that moves Deleuze closer to our concept of the imageless image. What's more, in Deleuze's early reading of archetypal theory as a theory of forces, we observe the Nietzschean inflections at odds with a more dialectical reading of Jung. With Nietzsche and Jung as mediators, the early Deleuze aligns himself with a view of the unconscious as a differential admixture irreducible to a properly "objective" content. "[T]here are very different levels of the unconscious, of unequal origin and value, arousing regressions which differ in nature, which have relations of opposition, compensation and reorganization going on between them."[34] Deleuze's nascent concept of the unconscious consists of a recombinatory logic governed by a fluctuation of energetic quantities over multiple registers of expression. At the intersection of Nietzschean and Jungian sensibilities, we might say that Deleuze's understanding of archetypal figurations becomes salient in virtue of quantitatively dominant unconscious valences. Deleuze's idea that forms of differencing unfold along multiple vectors and articulate themselves in accord with various forms of embodied constitutions provides us with an initial point of leverage to unsettle the premise of there being only one form or manner of individuation.

ONE OR MANY INDIVIDUATIONS?

As we abandon Freud's demand for an unconscious defined by its objectal polarities, we should apply an equal scrutiny towards the notion of archetypes. In what ways might the traditional image of thought loom large over Jung's ideas? What are the epistemological grounds for the existence of archetypes and the teleology of individuation? Another more specific question, however, takes us to the heart of the matter: what is the ontological notion (or fantasy) that most adequately encompasses our understanding of the individuation process: the many or the one? Like Deleuze and Guattari, Hillman believes the unexamined primacy of unity over multiplicity presents one of the eminent challenges of rethinking or relationship to images. Hillman problematizes one of the core tenets of Jung's theory of individuation: its monotheistic overcoding of the unconscious. To be sure, Hillman insists upon making a firm distinction between what he describes as a "monotheistic temperament" and existing monotheisms.[35] For Hillman, an historical inquiry into the primacy of existing monotheism fails to yield solid grounds that would explain how thought in the West has generally maintained a predisposition towards unifying themes and motifs. Even among various Western monotheisms, for example, there exist sectarian trends that exhibit a range of tendencies from doctrinaire to pluralistic. Nonetheless, Hillman acknowledges Jung's bias expressed unequivocally in *Aion*, where Jung asserts that "the anima/animus stage is correlated with polytheism, the self with monotheism."[36] Jung ultimately considers the agonies of the unconscious merely as a preliminary fodder for the ultimately unifying process of individuation. Hillman counters this view, pushing the logic of individuation to its limit:

If there is only one model of individuation can there be true individuality? The complexes that will not be integrated force recognition of their autonomous power. Their archetypal core will not serve the single goal of monotheistic wholeness.[37]

This implosion of the monistic model of individuation splinters into a possible multiplicity of individuations. Moreover, Hillman's more general criticism opens up possibilities for a more anarchic image of individuation, a non-recognitive image resistant to imposed forms of integration, a conception of the image with an affirmative disposition towards ambiguity. To be sure, Hillman indeed makes the case for a polytheistic psychologizing of images, but he does not do so to necessarily *resolve* opposing views. As for establishing the best idea of an individuation model, grounds of contestation are always pitched in favor of a unifying concept. Jung says as much in his psychological consideration of monism and pluralism.[38] He asserts that the monistic idea itself imposes its sovereignty upon the image — which is to say it overlays an image of itself upon other images. Hence, to restore life to images, we will advocate for imageless images!

The affirmation of a polytheistic psychology involutes the dominant attitudes of Freud and Jung, frustrating their shared demand for forms of "identity, unity, centeredness, [and] integration."[39] Hillman's polytheism does not directly disavow the fantasy of unity per se, but rather opens an aperture of experiences, which privileges "differentiating, elaborating, particularizing, complicating, affirming, and preserving." Hillman writes, "The emphasis is less upon changing what is there into something better (transformation and improvement) and more on deepening what is there into itself."[40] Here we achieve one of the goals of conceptualizing the imageless image by unsettling the implicit normativity of ontologically "correct" or "ideal" models. The ethical openness affirmed by Hillman is less about the formation of a conceptually sound ontology — a task he ascribes to theology — and is more akin to encouraging explorations between imagined ontological dispositions and the affective temperaments that positively guide those actually doing image work.

At this juncture, recalling our previous discussion of Deleuze's work in *Proust & Signs* becomes useful for rethinking the fantasy of unity in the context of image work. For Deleuze, the apprenticeship philosophical is itself a series of encounters with *signs* — or to interpolate in Hillman's terms, *images*. Deleuze articulates the experience of unity as those moments that enfold the non-philosophical moments of our lives with moments of consummating philosophical insight.[41] These events occur along the same continuum populated by all other experiences without subsuming or abolishing the particularities constitutive of the event. Put another way, Deleuze's conception of the epiphany of unity avoids putting multiplicity under erasure. Every moment of the philosophical apprenticeship, even the experience of unity itself, remains implicated in a broader array of multiple events.

To be sure, a pluralistic view of individuation does not simply expand the field of Oedipal objects. It rather affirms the irreducibility of any image to a set of reference points. We assert neither a correspondence theory of the image nor a coherentist view, but an altogether nonrepresentational approach. An apt example (or image) to better convey this irreducibility are the sculptures of Alexander Calder we know as "mobiles" (a term coined by Marcel Duchamp). Jungian scholar Stanton Marlan gestures to the kinetic image of Calder's mobile as a "provocative model" to elucidate the sublime complexities of the self.[42] However, Marlan's view of the image may presuppose the notion of a rarefied self in the place of that which is, in fact, proper to the image itself: complexity, perspectives, movements. Jean-Paul Sartre proffers his own view of Calder's work:

A mobile does not suggest anything: It captures genuine living movement and shapes them. Mobiles have no meaning, make you think of nothing but themselves. They are, that is all. [...] There is more of the unpredictable about them than any other human creation. [...] They are nevertheless it was lyrical inventions, technical contributions of them almost mathematical quality and sensitive symbols of nature [sic].[43]

What Sartre observes in the image of the mobile we similarly lift up about the life of images themselves. Meanings as static perspectives ultimately fail to circumscribe the mobile's aleatory quality. We should note that the vitality of the image is not inherently opposed or entirely fatal to meaning itself. However, to be certain, meanings can never stand in for the image as an encounter or an enactment. To posit a meaning adequate to the dynamism of the mobile image urges us to embrace the transience of a kind of perspectivism — meanings as multiple masks, ephemeral coalescences which both germinate and come to pass amidst the mobile's kinetic fluidity.

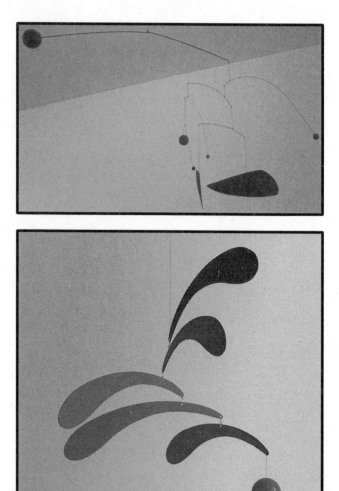

Above: Mobile, metal, wood, wire and string sculpture by Alexander Calder, c. 1932, Tate Modern
Below: Flowing Rhythm by Ole Flensted of Flendsted Mobiles in Denmark

THE ARCHETYPE AS A THRESHOLD OF POIETIC INSURGENCY

The idea of images as kinetics or a perspectivism of the image attends to an important basis for Hillman's rethinking (or clarification) of Jung's archetypes. For Hillman, the realm of the imaginal is an ecology of fantasies irreducible to any one among them. His model pre-empts the Jungian primacy of the ego-self dyad and its tendency to force other types of fantasies into the service of the self. Hillman rejects the imperialism of the ego-self dyad in part due to its overpronounced heroism. He lambastes the excesses of heroic fantasies, particularly those pervasive Western figures of the hero, such as the capitalist, the colonial despot, and the zealous professional. However, it is also the doctor and the psychoanalyst who adopt heroic paradigms and methodologies when they attempt to prune the body and imaginal of its pathologies. Cure seekers, such as psychoanalysts, employ allopathic methods of excision, aiming to arrest psychopathologies and appropriate them for the project of Herculean integration. Hillman instead urges us to develop an intimacy with our pathologies, a care which at once tends to the image itself and evokes sublime affects within the image's caregiver. During his early training as a psychoanalyst in Zürich, Hillman undertook a period of self-analysis in response to a persistent, overwhelming depression.[44] The images that arose during this period involved Hillman imaging himself diving into the ocean. He shuddered approaching the ocean's more ominous depths, a dark abyss populated by an invisible menagerie of sea creatures. Despite the trepidation aroused by these episodes of active imagination, he discovered that he was able to breathe underwater in the context of his reveries. This vital observation amidst the terror induced by the image created for Hillman the conditions for the possibility of transforming the whole tableau of his depression fantasy. The act of noticing the ability to breath aroused a deepening of the image. In Hillman's case, the deepening event did not invoke the heroism with which depression is often treated, i.e., attempting to negate or diminish symptoms qua symptom. Hillman believes that a heroic impulse suffuses those hermeneutical strategies that put interventions of the symbolic order before our sensitivity to the eventfulness of the image itself. Such methods serve to suppress the profound alterity of a fugue state and the potential richness of its transformative power.

Hillman's critique of the hero and his attendant displacement of the ego-function also raises the question of whether his theory of the image constitutes a significant break with Jung. Despite significant divergences from Jung's core concepts, Hillman nonetheless understands himself as faithful to Jung's conception of archetypes, especially as the concept was more thoroughly elaborated in Jung's later study. Hillman notes that the body of writings which follow the completion of Jung's *Liber Novus* (*The Red Book*) articulate a set of necessary distinctions, which disabuse us of the misconception that archetypes comprise static representational figurations. In *Psychological Types*, Jung explains that the primary function of the psyche is *to fantasize,* to create images and not merely to reflect or represent them.[45] At this juncture, Jung affirms that our modes of fantasizing are akin to poetic expression. Hillman extends this insight, positing that our work with images is not meant to escape complexes but to move towards them or more deeply into them. For Hillman, the fantasy is what gives the complex both its "form and elaboration."[46] We thus derive from Hillman a positive figure of escape, an involution, one which more intimately "involves" the image. To avoid any equivocation, what we escape is not the complex but the peremptory fantasy of the ego/self — that bourgeois delirium which incessantly demands tribute from the imagination. In the end, the archetype for Hillman is not a meaning but a threshold or a set of coordinates, which shows us where we are in relation to our complexes.

We can imagine this clarified conception of the archetypal image as a kind of poietic insurgency which irrupts through a shared semiotic crust, accreting from it particles that allow it to take shape. The vitality of the archetypal image grows in virtue of its transversal movement through various imagistic thresholds, escaping the determinations of meaning. It gathers up residues, ambiguities, fragments, and bricolage in an event of radical differentiation.

When exploring the contours of an image as it is presented in a fantasy, we may find familiar forms or resemblances which provoke interpretation. However, a risk lies in simply reducing what appears to symbols or types. Hillman remarks that "Types call for living instances [...] this peculiar process of thought — the need for examples — cast a shadow over all uses of typological thinking, especially in psychology and psychiatry."[47] He acknowledges the tendency of typologies and symbologies to extort from life verisimilitude at the expense of life as it is lived. A typically binaristic construction of types tends towards eclipsing the lively ambiguities that constitute images. Symbolic reductions, in particular, foreclose upon what immediately becomes present in an image. "Typologies fascinate and convince," Hillman writes, "because they are methods of mirroring what we must look for — self-perception, recognition of our individual image."[48] Our desire for recognition in our interpretation of images thus remains prone to a paranoiac tendency. It derives from an impulse to barter away living images in exchange for the solidity of ossified meanings. One may rather wager a sense of completeness, finding out what their fantasies *mean* versus taking on the ambiguous task of finding out *what they are doing*. In other words, there is a *fascisizing* potential in our fascination with reductive schemas, which prefer an image's transcendent identity over its immanent potency. Ultimately, for Hillman, the intervention of the symbol or type "disturbs our appreciation of the image and our ability to imagine."[49] In any case, symbols and types cannot exhaust the imagination. Gaston Bachelard, an important mediator in Hillman's work, puts a finer point on the matter:

> Imagination eludes the determinations of psychology, psychoanalysis included — and that it constitutes an autochthonous, autogenous realm. We subscribe to this view: rather than the will, rather than the *élan vital*, Imagination is the true source of psychic production. Psychically, we are created by our reverie — created and limited by our reverie — for it is the reverie which delineates the furthest limits of our mind.[50]

In our pursuit of the imageless image, we find Bachelard's speculative autogeny of the image a useful milestone: the prospect of cultivating an imagination capable of outstripping typological determinations and affirming itself as its own generative locus. The vitality of the image resides within overcoming those determinations which prefigure its essence. Hence, for Hillman, to retain what's proper to the image, we endeavor to "stick to it" as its own non-reified, lively event.

"Sticking with the image," for Hillman, involves a qualitative shift in our attention, one keen on *noticing and supposing* versus *prefiguring or presupposing*. We find perhaps the strongest distillation of the concept of sticking with the image in an episode of dream analysis that took place between Hillman and one of his patients. In a dream that featured the image of a black snake, Hillman urges the dreamer to "keep the snake" and not sacrifice the image to an interpretation. He writes:

> the moment you've defined the snake, interpreted it, you've lost the snake, you've stopped it and the person leaves the hour with a concept about my repressed sexuality or my cold black passions ... and you've lost the snake. The task of analysis is to keep the snake there, the black snake ... see, the black snake's no longer necessary the moment it's been interpreted, and you don't need your dreams anymore because they've been interpreted.[51]

Similarly, when we presuppose the overlay of Oedipus or the totality of an ego/self, we tend to filter important differences present in the actual image. In Hillman's view, these differences occur at the level of intensity: in observing the distinct hue of a shade of red, for example, or by experiencing a unique convergence of visual and aural stimuli — i.e., the sound of a crow when a child opens its mouth. Hillman indicates that the process of active selection of details allows us to then "suppose" things about an image (versus presupposing them) that compel us towards a practice of *active imagination*.[52] We stay with the image by working with and within the salient details of its event — in other words, by locating its internal tensions and developing a dialogue with points of interest. Additionally, by taking up "metaphorical attitude," we cultivate an ability Hillman calls "seeing-through."[53] Seeing-though pierces the epistemological veneer spread over the forces and elements that structure experience in order to apprehend their constitutive intensities. By intentionally heightening our sensitivity to images, we can then begin to locate "archetypal dominants," or the archetypal fantasies that predominate in a given fantasy. Though Hillman advises the use of metaphors, he employs them primarily to explore tensions provoked by phenomenological experimentation. The essence of his method is to engender the careful sensitivity and discerning acumen of a ship captain:

> Think of when you are sailing. You are never on course. You are always correcting. Only through these constant corrections do you find your course. You need to ask yourself, "Am I too personal here, thinking only of my own 'growth'? Am I too much like a 'missionary' there, bringing 'light' to these people?" The movement, movement through it, is part of the essence. [...] At any moment as you travel on a circle you can think, "I got it." You fix on the point and can easily go off on a tangent. The plan is the sensitivity...[54]

At this juncture, it is worthwhile to recognize how Hillman's influence has unsettled views of traditional therapy and ushered the practice of image work into communal spaces. Activists and organizers who are also enthusiasts of Hillman's ideas have created new forms of engaged practice. Archetypal psychologist Mary Watkins, for instance, catalogs a host of ecological activism involving the collective sharing of fantasies, associations, *notitia* (what we notice in episodes of active noticing), and dialogues to inspire political action around ecological and biodiversity issues. In these settings, group fabulations comprise their own agon of imagery, evoking discussions around local issues, such as public uses of land and the impact of human dwelling on other forms of life. These meditations elicit various intensities of feeling and acts of fantasizing, which then fall back upon various forms of community action. At its core, this type of work instigates a challenge to the paternalistic dynamics of early psychoanalysis and some of its depoliticizing tendencies.

BECOMING BEYOND METAPHOR

Metaphors instigate the centripetal force of signs, which draw images into black holes. The refusal of metaphor demands a different kind of movement in relation to the image: a vortical movement spawned in conjunction with the image, a set of mutualized motilities, a localized eddy of intensities formulated in a series of intimate responses (as with active imagination). When we are compelled by certain images or overcome by a particularly powerful fantasy, we are swept up in a complex set of forces we are "lived by" but that we often fail to understand, as Auden says. Images often arise at the fringe of our conscious delirium to announce a collective desire whose event exceeds any likeness to anything already in our purview. One of the basic tenets we will continue to emphasize is how an understanding of images as metaphors brings to bear as the basis of a political ontology we ferociously resist: that a form of life or a life experienced in its radical singularity must ultimately reduce to an intelligible category in the symbolic order before its importance can be realized. The images do not arrive as an impetus for an act of confession made to the symbolic order, but as potential collaborators in acts of political enunciation. To break with metaphor is to affirm a greater abstractness of the image and to create the conditions for comprehending its entanglement with the broader field of political desire. While our encounter with the image is seemingly staged at a phenomenal threshold, the encounter is irreducible to phenomenology as such. The affirmation of the phenomenal immediacy of the image, an intimacy with the image as presented in the purview of experience, opens a space in which a holistic transformation of our sense of relationality to both images and ourselves becomes possible.

There is an important conceptual overlap between the radical relationality towards images proffered by Hillman and the concept of becoming (becoming-animal, becoming-woman, becoming-child, etc.) in the work of Deleuze and Guattari. In Hillman's attempt to advance a nonrepresentational concept of the image, we see him reaching for his own theory of becomings, images *as* becomings. In any case, identifying the junctures where both Hillman and Deleuze and Guattari consider our relationship with animals or our encounter with the animal-image is perhaps the most apt way to thread the needle we have called the imageless image. We must, however, somewhat pre-empt the convergence by acknowledging Hillman's commitment to metaphor or "the metaphorical attitude" as an incipient disposition to engage in transformative image work. Putting that aside, we conclude our philosophy of fugitive images with *becoming-animal* and *becoming-sorcerer* as meditations of escape.

For Deleuze and Guattari, becoming-animal is a type of becoming that refers to the collapse of the insistent solidity of our human identity in conjunction with an embodiment that occurs in virtue of our relationship to animality. Typically, the capacity of our vital expression as living beings exceeds what has ordinarily been delimited as "human" by the dominant, rational social order. On the other hand, our relationship with animals, whether it is with actual animals or the animals we encounter in our dreams or fantasies, involves exposing the transformative liminality between a certain rational and non-rational dimension of our experience. Deleuze and Guattari suggest that various approximations of animality can unsettle our otherwise limiting human-centric tendencies. Their view also echoes Georges Bataille's call to evoke the "lost intimacy" of animality, the provenance of an affective richness abandoned in our collective assent to the dictates of civility. Overcoming this separation of ourselves from these tendencies involves an act of creative involution, an embodiment of characteristics and perspectives alien to the civil creature. Becoming-animal is thus a blurring or deactivation of the presupposition of the man-animal binary. For Deleuze and Guattari, this critical maneuver produces a *release* which creates waves of affective resonances, which populate intensities along a vector that runs between human and animal.

More broadly, Deleuze and Guattari's theory of becomings asserts that the binary oppositions found in configurations such as man-woman, man-child, and man-animal presuppose a linkage between the terms that is ultimately "imaginary" in the sense that they are socially constructed, i.e., that their efficacy is not independent of the social and political structures that produce and reinforce them. The construction of binaries not only divests the subordinate or *minor* pole of its importance ontologically, but also relegates its energetic potencies. Much like Hillman's treatment of images, becomings are not a reduction of terms to a matter of polar opposites — they are the inward folding of these poles. Hence becoming is a creative involution that entails "involving" terms in *blocks* (as opposed to strict linear axes), that run their "own line 'between' the terms in play and beneath assignable relations."[55] The dominant term in image binaries maintains an appropriative function insofar as the binarism remains operative. However, by occupying the minor pole in a becoming, to affirm its *minor becoming*, we are able to unsettle the binary configuration and tunnel out from beneath it. In the case of becoming-animal, Deleuze and Guattari write that one "does not 'really' become an animal any more than the animal 'really' becomes something else. Becoming produces nothing other than itself."[56] Becoming-animal, once again, is the formulation of a "middle" between human and animal, a relational space evocative of intensities, affects, and movement — a becoming-*other*.

Alongside the process of becoming-animal, Deleuze

and Guattari also confer a special importance to the figure of the sorcerer, or the form of embodiment they call *becoming-sorcerer*.[57] Unlike the dominant figures of myth, whose roles and functions have been inscribed deep into the archetypal schema, the sorcerer of tales and folklore remains a scandal, haunting the edges of towns and villages, occupying liminal dwellings, roaming rustic borderlands, and practicing a secret arcanum. The "truth" of the sorcerer is always muddled in hearsay or gossip, and, unlike the gods, the extent of their powers and alliances remains shrouded in secrecy. Much like Porete, they live in a constant state of refusal; their existence menaces the state and the ocular apparatuses of constituent power, which ceaselessly attempt to reintegrate marginal subjects. To engender the becomings of the sorcerer is to become a political aberration. The figure of the sorcerer evades the domesticating stamp of the filiative apparatuses within the social order while instead propagating illicit alliances and clandestine networks at the fringes. These alliances skirt the appropriative mechanisms of social recording, becoming imperceptible and insulating themselves within *a sacred conspiracy*. Porete, the heretic, became a kind of sorcerer. Hers was a conspiracy of an inner multitude, allied only with the divine images which scintillated in her heart. To be sure, the politics of becoming-sorcerer eschews the grandiosity of myth, instead engendering an elusive, folkloric character. Rumors of sorcery are less magnanimous legends than apocryphal tales disseminated in whispers. Becoming-sorcerer is not only the paradigmatic becoming of escape, but also perhaps the figure of becoming most troubling to the dogmatic image of thought. The deceptive sorcerer lives as a perennial antagonist for what is deemed true, good, and common. Theirs is a worldly alchemy intent upon furtively crafting its homunculi from a septic flesh of resistance, one sworn to scalding the hand of the inquisitor and profaning his holy touch. To be clear, our invocation of the sorcerer's rebellion is by no means gratuitous nor is it meant to be superfluously avant-garde. What is at stake remains apparent: the philter of capitalist desire has spilt forth history's darkest enchantment, a seemingly interminable spell in which all race to drown in the swirl of capital's euphoric malaise. Becoming-sorcerer entails the prospect of finding a counter-enchantment, a new ardor to propel us out of hell.

CONCLUDING UN-CYBERNETIC POSTSCRIPT: WHAT IS PHILOSOPHY?

The image of Hell, at first glance, appears to be an unwelcome visitor to the discussion of psychosocial machines. Nonetheless, the machinic economy of the image and of the unconscious, in being determined by the capitalist process, tends towards an infinite and unyielding drive for accumulation and production. The law of value has instituted itself in the world-system as its Imperial axiom. With the help of many of the machineries we have taken great pains to describe, it has achieved a perfect isomorphism with that legal institution that, according to dominant trends in Christian theology, "knows neither interruption nor end: Hell."[1] The image of Hell is isomorphic, translatable in form and function, to the principle of the world-system. Such an image of eternal Hellfire is nonetheless not an ahistorical image, but an image whose popularity has bloomed under a Calvinist, capitalist unconscious centered on an eternally decreed and unyielding debt. Namely, the debt of systems to perpetually correct their course in infinite gatherings of feedback and data, and the debt that capital owes to itself, the imperative to always be more of itself, to *capitalize* on itself.

One does not escape Hell by redemption — itself an economic transaction — but through a rendering inoperative of the infernal economy. The question is not, in a sense, "what" is to be done, but "*how* is it to be done." It is a matter of tactics in relation to an understanding of the enemy's machinery and their points of strategic oversight. Whether it is Mackandal in Haiti, the George Floyd Rebellion, the Toul prison rioters, the resistance of groups like ADAPT, or Porete's silence before the inquisitor, each provides an exemplar of a maneuver of escape, a withdrawal made in order to make possible a means of counterattack. The withdrawal that makes new becomings possible, which is also an assault on what is, *that* is creative involution.

Withdrawal is nonetheless a matter of degree in our increasingly cybernated world, with capture around every corner, and a precarious working life ever more common. It seems impossible to embrace the kinds of fugitivity of a Mackandal, nor can we all withdraw in the manner of the popular image of escaping the cities to rural homesteads. Nonetheless, what is to be withdrawn from is the ceaseless motion and flow of capitalist production and cybernetic governance. One can withdraw from *within*, much like the creative involution of an organ. It is only in the secrecy of tactical moments of withdrawal *within* the systems that we can find each other — at a pub, at a union meeting, or in conspiratorial spaces. The first task is theorizing, then strategizing. We do not believe we have communicated any kind of totality of machines, and the *Cybercene* may yet bequeath to us more horrors; nonetheless, we have presented machines that operate as the apparatuses, which determine so many contours of our current inferno.

At this point, it may be expected that we will make the typical gesture of a denunciation of philosophy as a kind of pseudo-activity:

"We philosophers have only interpreted the world-system, but it is up to you, The People, to change it."

No.

This platitude suggests a distance that philosophy constantly occupies, and which we categorically refuse. As we assert in the beginning, we assert at the end: every text, and therefore every philosophy, is a machine, always involved with the community it establishes with its audience, and the theoretical and political desires that connect the two. Philosophy cannot stand detached from the world, and any claim that it could is a false pretense that only functions to detach it from its own collaboration with the world as it currently is.

Philosophy is the creation of concepts in a manner *hostile* to the order of things, or it is mere collaboration with it.

NOTES

THE CYBERPUNK PRESENT
1 Sadie Plant, *Zeros and Ones*, (Fourth Estate, 1997), 181.
2 Gerald Raunig, *Dissemblage*, (Minor Compositions, 2022), 11.
3 Ambalavaner Sivanandan, "New Circuits of Imperialism" in *Communities of Resistance*, (Verso, 2019), pp. 169–195, 189–90.
4 Mark Fisher, *Flatline Constructs*, (Exmilitary, 2018), 22.
5 Sivanandan, "All That Melts into Air is Solid" in *Communities of Resistance*, (Verso, 2019), pp.19–59, 42.
6 Ian Alan Paul, *Are Prisons Computers?*, www.ianalanpaul.com/are-prisons-computers/
7 Ibid.
1 Georges Bataille, *The Accursed Share, Volume 1*, (Zone, 1988), 59.

BURN YOUR WAY OUT: THE CYBERNETICS OF REVOLT
2 Gilles Deleuze and Félix Guattari, *A Thousand Plateaus*, (Bloomsbury, 2018), 509.
3 Tiqqun, *The Cybernetic Hypothesis*, 122.
4 Ibid., 121.
5 Ibid., 39–40.
6 Jay W. Forrester, *Principles of Systems*, (Wright-Allen, 1968), 5.
7 Ibid.
8 Norbert Wiener, *Cybernetics*, (MIT, 2019), 61.
9 Forrester, *Principles of Systems*, 5.

10 F.H. George, *Cybernetics in Management*, (Pan, 1970), 51.

11 Sadie Plant and Nick Land, "Cyberpositive," in *#ACCELERATE: The Accelerationist Reader*, (Urbanomic, 2017), edited by Robin Mackay and Armen Avanessian, pp. 304–313, 305.

12 Tiqqun, *The Cybernetic Hypothesis*, 24.

13 George, *Cybernetics in Management*, 4.

14 Stafford Beer, *Cybernetics and Management* (The English Universities Press, 1959), 25.

15 Deleuze and Guattari, *A Thousand Plateaus*, 509.

16 Ibid.

17 Immanuel Kant, *Critique of Pure Reason*, (Palgrave Macmillan, 2003), A569/B597.

18 Tiqqun, *The Cybernetic Hypothesis*, 25.

19 Achille Mbembe, *Necropolitics*, (Duke, 2019), 66.

20 Giorgio Agamben, *What is an Apparatus?*, (Stanford, 2009), 8.

21 Idris Robinson, "How Might it Should be Done," *Ill Will*, https://illwill.com/how-it-might-should-be-done

22 Abigail Weinberg, "Nancy Pelosi Thanks George Floyd for 'Sacrificing' Himself by Being Killed by the Police," *Mother Jones*, https://www.motherjones.com/politics/2021/04/nancy-pelosi-thanks-george-floyd-for-the-sacrifice-of-being-killed-by-the-police/

23 Saul Newman, "What is an Insurrection? Destituent Power and Ontological Anarchy in Agamben and Stirner," *Political Studies,* Vol. 65: 2, (2017), pp. 284–299, 288.

24 Sivanandan, "All that Melts into Air is Solid," 19–59, 57.

25 Karl Marx and Friedrich Engels, *Collected Works Volume 5: Marx and Engels 1845–1847*, (Lawrence and Wishart, 2010), 49. Given that this line was written in response to Stirner, a man who thought that communism would not abolish *enough* institutions, no Leninist philology regarding the manifold sense of the German *Aufhebung* in this or in

various texts can offset the annihilation of the world (or the capitalist use thereof) demanded in this passage.

26 George, *Cybernetics in Management*, 43.

27 Gilles Deleuze, *Two Regimes of Madness*, (MIT, 2003), 322.

28 Andrew Neal, Sven Opitz, and Chris Zebrowski, "Capturing Protest in Urban Environments. The 'Police Kettle' As a Territorial Strategy," *EPD: Society and Space* (2019), Vol. 37(6), 1045–1063, 1046.

29 Ibid.

30 Ibid, 1053.

31 Ibid.

32 Ibid., 1054.

33 Ibid.

34 Ibid., 1055.

35 Ibid., 1057.

36 Phil Jones, *Work without the Worker*, (Verso, 2021), 68.

37 Resources on how to start an Anti-Raids group can be found here: http://antiraids.net/wp-content/uploads/2016/04/anti-raids-zine.pdf

38 Silvia Federici, *Caliban and the Witch*, (Autonomedia, 2004), 97.

39 These lines are delivered in a short, pay-as-you-want video game by Colestia, *A Bewitching Revolution*, about detaching from and revolting against the circuits of neoliberal cyber capitalism. As a consciousness-raising tool, it is indisputably beautiful for the sense of hope and emancipatory agency that it restores to the player. You can acquire it here: https://colestia.itch.io/a-bewitching-revolution

40 M.E. O'Brien, *Communizing Care*, https://pinko.online/pinko-1/communizing-care

41 Tiqqun, *The Cybernetic Hypothesis*, 25.

42 Graffiti from the wall of the subway system in *A Bewitching Revolution* during the titular revolt.

43 Fred Moten, *In the Break*, (Minnesota, 2003), 21–22.

COUNTER-INSURGENCY OF THE EYE: A MANUAL FOR THE PRACTICE OF OCULARITY

1 Andrew Culp, *A Guerrilla Guide to Refusal,* (Minnesota, 2022), 32.

2 Ibid.

3 Deleuze and Guattari, *A Thousand Plateaus*, 427.

4 Guéry and Deleule, *The Productive Body*, (Zer0, 2014), 57–8.

5 U.S. Army Field Manual *FM3-24/MCWP 3-33.5: Insurgencies and Countering Insurgencies*, (2014) Chapter 7 Section 7, https://fas.org/irp/doddir/army/fm3-24.pdf

6 C. Paul, C.P. Clarke, B. Grill, and M. Dunigan, *Paths to Victory,* (RAND, 2013), 173.

7 Robinson, "How Might it Should be Done".

8 Gilles Deleuze, *Nietzsche and Philosophy,* (Athlone, 1983), 3–4.

9 Deleuze and Guattari, *A Thousand Plateaus,* 421–422.

10 Tiqqun, *Introduction to Civil War,* (Semiotext(e), 2010), 205.

11 G.W.F. Hegel, *Phenomenology of Spirit*, (Oxford, 1977), Section 109.

12 Ibid., Section 490.

13 Shelley Tremain, "This Is What a Historicist and Relativist Feminist Philosophy of Disability Looks Like," in *Foucault Studies*, Vol. 19, pp. 7–42 (2015), 16.

14 Hegel, *Phenomenology of Spirit*, Sections 589–595.

15 See: Geoffrey Demarest (US Army Foreign Studies Office, Fort Leavenworth), "Geopolitics and Urban Armed Conflict in Latin America" in *Small Wars and Insurgencies*, Vol. 6, No. 1 (Routledge, 1995). This point of ocularity strategy has been recognized and recorded by certain conspiratorial elements. (See Anon., *Desert*, (Active Distribution, 2011), 51).

16 Catherine Malabou, *Ontology of the Accident,* (Polity, 2012), 23.

17 Ibid., 22.

18 Ibid.

19 Ocularity is hence a transcendental logic in the Kantian sense, and Kant ought to be recognized as an ocular pioneer.

20 Malabou, *Ontology of the Accident,* 90.

21 Gilles Deleuze and Félix Guattari, *Anti-Oedipus*, (Minnesota, 1983), 78–79.

22 Mark Fisher, *Capitalist Realism*, (Zer0, 2009), 21.

23 Jules Joanne Gleeson and Elle O'Rourke, "Introduction," in *Transgender Marxism*, (Pluto, 2021), pp. 1–32, 24.

24 Michel Foucault, *Herculine Barbin*, (Vintage, 2010), vii.

25 Ibid.

26 Ibid., viii-ix.

27 Michel Foucault, *Abnormal: Lectures at the College de France 1974–1975.* (G. Burchell, Trans.) (Picador, 2003), 64–5.

28 Paul B. Preciado, *Can the Monster Speak?*, (Fitzcarraldo, 2021), 35.

29 Kathryn Pauly Morgan, "Gender Police," in *Foucault and the Government of Disability*, (Michigan, 2005) , pp. 298–328, 299.

30 Ibid., 301.

31 Jordy Rosenberg, "Afterword: One Utopia, One Dystopia" in: *Transgender Marxism* (Pluto, 2021), pp. 259–295, 286.

32 Sandy O' Sullivan, "The Colonial Project of Gender (and Everything Else)" in: *Genealogy*, Vol. 5. No. 67, (2021), pp. 1–9, 3–4.

33 Morgan Carpenter, *Intersex: Intersectionalities with Disabled People*, (2020), https://ihra.org.au/21214/intersex-and-disability/

34 Judith Butler, "Can One Lead a Good Life in a Bad Life?", *Radical Philosophy*, (2012), https://www.radicalphilosophy. com/article/can-one-lead-a-good-life-in-a-bad-life

35 Henri-Jacques Stiker, *The History of Disability*, (Michigan, 2019), 128.

36 Ibid., 125.

37 Ibid.

38 Ibid., 136.

39 Martin Sullivan, "Subjected Bodies: Paraplegia, Rehabilitation, and the Politics of Movement," in: *Foucault and the Government of Disability*, (Michigan, 2005), pp. 27–44, 36.

40 Kant, *Critique of Pure Reason*, Bxvi.

41 Gilles Deleuze, "Postscript on the Societies of Control" in *October* Vol. 59 (1992),. 3–7, 7.

42 Stiker, *The History of Disability*, 130.

43 Deleuze, "Postscript on the Societies of Control", 3–7, 6.

44 For an extensive study, see: Frances Ryan, *Crippled: Austerity and the Demonization of Disabled People*, (Verso, 2019).

45 Stiker, *The History of Disability*, 132.

46 Ruth Wilson Gilmore, *Abolition Geography*, (Verso, 2022), 264–5.

47 Lewis Gordon, *What Fanon Said*, (Fordham, 2015), 136.

48 Ibid.

49 Cedric J. Robinson, *Black Marxism*, (Penguin, 2020), 9.

50 Ibid., 27–8.

51 Ibid., 10.

52 Charles W. Mills, *Blackness Visible: Essays on Philosophy and Race*, (Cornell, 1998), 46.

53 Michael Banton, "The Classification of Races in Europe and North America: 1700–1850," in: *Race and Racialization: Essential Readings*, eds. Tania Das Gupta, Carl E. James, Chris Andersen, Grace-Edward Galabuzi, and Roger C.A. Maaka, (Canadian Scholars, 2018), 25–35, 27.

54 Hegel, *Phenomenology of Spirit*, Section 343.

55 Kieron Smith, *The Politics of Down Syndrome*, (Zer0, 2010), 12.

56 Ibid., 12–13.

57 For an example of the perseverance of such post-scientific ocular meanings persevering into practice as social mythology, see: Hoffman, Kelly M, et al. "Racial bias in pain assessment and treatment recommendations, and false beliefs about biological differences between blacks and whites," *Proceedings of the National Academy of Sciences of the United States of America*, Vol. 113, 16 (2016), 4296–301.

58 Mills, *Blackness Visible: Essays on Philosophy and Race*, 56.

59 Ibid.

60 Robinson, *Black Marxism*, 81.

61 Moten, *In the Break*, 16.

62 Robinson, *Black Marxism*, 81.

63 G.W.F. Hegel, *Philosophy of Mind*, (Oxford, 2010), 41.

64 Robinson, *Black Marxism*, 82.

65 Ibid.

66 Karl Marx, *Capital*, Volume I, (Penguin, 1990), 874.

67 Robinson, *Black Marxism*, 121–2.

68 Ibid., 136–7.

69 Michael Craton, *Sinews of Empire*, Anchor, (Garden City), 1974, 218; and also Patterson, *The Sociology of Slavery*, (Fairleigh Dickenson, 1969), 185–95, cited in: Ibid., 136.

70 Ibid., 136.

71 Ibid., 169.

72 Francis Heylighen and Cliff Joslyn, "Cybernetics and Second Order Cybernetics" in: *Encyclopedia of Physical Science and Technology*, v.4, (2003), ed. R.A. Meyers, 155–170, 165.

73 Ibid.

74 The recognition of this double-bind of species-categorization has been identified previously by insurgent forces, whose response to Anthropological ocularity was to assert themselves on the side of the errant abnormality

that feedback aims to counteract. This required refusing all subsumption and identity in favor of an actively *insecure* consumption of the material world and its objects as "Unique" and *de facto* inexhaustible under ocular categories. Previous agents, such as Ernst Schultz, attempted to ocularize the insurgent Johann Kaspar Schmidt in the decades following this prescient outburst of his:

The inhuman is the actual, what exists on all sides, and through his proof that it is "inhuman" the critic only clearly expresses the tautological proposition that it is inhuman.

But what if the inhuman, in turning its back on itself with resolute courage, also turned away from the worrisome critic and left him standing, untouched and unaffected by his objections? "You call me the inhuman," it might say to him, "and I really am so — for you; but I am so only because you bring me into opposition with the human, and I could only despise myself so long as I let myself be bewitched by this opposition; I was despicable because I sought my 'better self' outside myself; I was the inhuman because I dreamed of the 'human'; I was like the pious who hunger after their 'true *I*' and always remain 'poor sinners'; I thought of myself only in comparison to another; enough, I was not all in all, was not — *unique*. But now I cease to appear to myself as inhuman, cease to measure myself and let myself be measured by the human, cease to recognized anything over me; and therefore — God bless, humane critic! I have only been the inhuman, am now I am no longer this, but am the unique, indeed, to your disgust, the egoistic, but the egoistic not as it lets itself be measured by the human, humane and unselfish, but the egoistic as the — unique. (Max Stirner, *The Unique and Its Property*, (Underworld Amusements, 2017), 163.)

Schultz partially succeeded in medicalizing Schmidt as a
case of paranoiac psychosis in 1903 after certain Marxist
elements failed to take care of him, and we at I.R.I.S. hope
this sticks.

75 R.D. Laing, *The Divided Self*, (Penguin, 2010), 39.

76 Ibid., 36.

77 Ibid., 44.

78 Ibid., 45.

79 See: Jason Read, "The Order and Connection of Ideology
is the same as the Order and Connection of Exploitation:
Or, Towards a Bestiary of the Capitalist Imagination,"
Philosophy Today, Vol. 59 (2), 175–189, 180.

GOING ASTRAY

1 Michel Foucault, "Life: Experience and Science," in: J.
Faubion (ed.), *The Essential Works of Foucault, 1954–1984:
Aesthetics, Method, and Epistemology,* (New York: The New
Press, 1993), 476.

2 Giorgio Agamben, "Absolute Immanence," in: *Potentialities:
Collected Essays in Philosophy*, (D. Heller-Roazen, trans),
(Stanford 1999), 221.

3 Foucault, *Abnormal*, 318.

4 See: G. Peters, MAiD – Marginalized Against
Institutionalizing Death – The Opposition to the Expansion
of MAiD is about faith – but just not the religious kind. –
mssinenomineblog (wordpress.com)/

5 Remi Kohler, "Nicolas Andry de Bois-Regard (Lyon 1658–
Paris 1742): The Inventor of the Word 'Orthopaedics'
and the Father of Parasitology," *Journal of Children's
Orthopaedics: Official Journal of the European Paediatric
Orthopaedic Society (EPOS)* 4 (4), (2010), 349.

6 Michel Foucault, *The Punitive Society: Lectures at the
College de France 1972–1973.* (G. Burchell, Trans.) (New
York: Picador, 2015), 238.

7 Julien Offray de La Mettrie, *Man A Machine and Man a Plant.* (R. Watson and N. Rybalka, Trans.), (Indianapolis: Hackett Publishing, 1994), 29.

8 Michel Foucault, *Discipline & Punish: The Birth of the Prison.* (A. Sheridan, Trans.) (New York: Pantheon Books, 1977), 137.

9 Georges Canguilhem, *The Normal and the Pathological.* (C. Fawcett, Trans.) (New York: Zone Books, 1989), 239.

10 Foucault, *Abnormal*, 50.

11 Michel Foucault, *"Society Must Be Defended": Lectures at the College de France 1975–1976.* (D. Macey, Trans.) (New York: Picador, 2003), 254.

12 Michel Foucault, *Security, Territory, Population: Lectures at the College de France 1977–1978.* (G. Burchell, Trans.) (New York: Picador, 2007), 169.

13 Stiker, *The History of Disability*, 26.

14 Foucault, *Security, Territory, Population,* 260.

15 Foucault, *Abnormal*, 318.

16 J.E. Wallin, *The Education of Handicapped Children.* (New York: The Riverside Press, 1924), 18.

17 Michel Foucault *Psychiatric Power: Lectures at the College de France 1973–1974.* (G. Burchell, Trans.) (New York: Picador, 2006), 210.

18 Ibid., 212.

19 Édouard Séguin, *Idiocy: And its Treatment by the Physiological Method*, (New York: New York Printing Company, 1866), 239.

20 Ibid., 65.

21 Ibid., 239.

22 Ibid., 83–84.

23 Ibid., 287.

24 Ibid., 73.

25 Ibid., 69.

26 Ibid., 70.

27 Wallin, *The Education of Handicapped Children*, 19.

28 Foucault, *Abnormal*, 154.

29 Foucault, *The Punitive Society*, 45.

30 Guillaume Le Trosne, *Mémoire sur les vagabonds et sur les mendiants.* (Paris: P.G. Simon, 1764), 9. (Author's translation).

31 Michel Foucault, *Madness & Civilization: A History of Insanity in the Age of Reason.* (R. Howard, Trans.) (New York: Pantheon Books, 1965), 50.

32 Ibid., 52.

33 Ibid., 67.

34 Foucault, *The Punitive Society*, 55.

35 Ibid., 173–174.

36 Ibid., 191.

37 Ibid., 196.

38 Michel Foucault, *Foucault Live: Collected Interviews, 1961–1984.* (L. Hochroth and J. Johnston, Trans.) (South Pasadena: Semiotext(e), 1989), 92–93.

39 Foucault, *Discipline & Punish,* 290–291.

40 Georges Bataille, *Inner Experience.* (S. Kendall, Trans.) (Albany: State University of New York Press, 2014) 47.

41 Foucault, *The Punitive Society*, 6.

42 Michel Foucault, *Power/Knowledge: Selections and Interviews 1972–1977.* (C. Gordon, L. Marshall, J. Mepham, K. Soper, Trans.) (New York: Pantheon, 1980), 180.

43 Nikolai Fedorov, "The Common Task," in *#ACCELERATE: The Accelerationist Reader*, (Robin Mackay and Armen Avanessian, eds.) (Urbanomic, 2017), 90.

44 Michel Foucault, *Psychiatric Power: Lectures at the College de France 1973–1974.* (G. Burchell, Trans.) (New York: Picador, 2006), 233.

45 Ibid., 307.

46 Michel Foucault, "To Escape Their Prison," in: K. Thompson, P. Zurn, eds., *Intolerable: Writings from Michel Foucault and the Prisons Information Group (1970–1980).* (Minneapolis: Minnesota University Press, 2021), 234.

47 Michel Foucault, "The Toul Speech," in: Ibid., 252.

48 Michel Foucault, "To Escape Their Prison," 235.

49 Ibid., 236.

50 Danika Worthington, "Meet the Disabled Activists from Denver who Changed a Nation," *Denver Post*. July 5, 2017.

51 Tiqqun, *This Is Not a Program*. (J. Jordan, Trans.), (South Pasadena: Semiotext(e), 2011), 152.

52 Andrew Culp, "Confronting Connectivity: Feminist Challenges to the Metropolis," *Communication and Critical Cultural Studies*. 13(2), (2016), 168.

53 The Invisible Committee, *To Our Friends*. (R. Hurley, Trans.) (South Pasadena: Semiotext(e), 2016), 183–184.

54 Giorgio Agamben, *Homo Sacer: Sovereign Power and Bare Life,* (D. Heller-Roazen, Trans.) (Stanford: Stanford University Press, 1998), 53.

55 Gilles Deleuze, "What is a Creative Act?" in: D. Lapoujade, ed., *Two Regimes of Madness: Texts and Interviews 1975–1995*, (South Pasadena: Semiotext(e), 2007), 327.

56 Giorgio Agamben, *When the House Burns Down*, (K. Attell, Trans.) (New York: Seagull Books, 2022), 78.

57 Michel Foucault, *The Courage of Truth (The Government of the Self and Others II): Lectures at the College de France 1983–1984*. (G. Burchell, Trans.) (New York: Picador, 2011), 314.

THE IMAGELESS IMAGE

1 Gilles Deleuze, "The Mystery of Ariadne According to Nietzsche," in: *Essays Critical and Clinical*, (The University of Minnesota Press 1997), 100.

2 Gilles Deleuze, "The Image of Thought," *Difference and Repetition*, (Columbia University Press 1994), 129–167.

3 For a relevant discussion, see: Acid Horizon, "Mark Fisher and Postcapitalist Desire: *Egress* with Matt Colquhoun," published July 3, 2020: https://www.youtube.com/watch?v=N9soC3RHubo

4 Gilles Deleuze, *Nietzsche & Philosophy*, (Columbia University Press 1983), xx.

5 Alan Schrift, "Nietzsche and the Critique of Oppositional Thinking" in *History of European Ideas*, Vol. 11 (Pergamon Press 1990), 785.

6 Gilles Deleuze, *Proust and Signs*, (University of Minnesota Press 2004).

7 Daniel W Smith, "Five Deleuzian Concepts," *Essays on Deleuze*, (Edinburgh University Press 1998), 198.

8 This explication derives its terms from the translator's preface in Deleuze's *Expressionism in Philosophy: Spinoza*. (See: Gilles Deleuze, *Expressionism in Philosophy: Spinoza*, Translated by Martin Joughin, (Zone Books 1992), 5–6.)

9 Deleuze and Guattari, *A Thousand Plateaus*, 318–19.

10 Gilles Deleuze and Claire Parnet, *Dialogues II*, (Columbia 2007), 110.

11 Ibid.

12 Ibid., 111.

13 Gilles Deleuze, "Doubts About the Imaginary," *Negotiations*, (Columbia University Press; Revised edition 1987).

14 This liberal recasting of Deleuze's epistemology is indebted to the work of Daniel W Smith. (See: Daniel W Smith, "Analytics: On the Becoming of Concepts," *Essays on Deleuze*, (Edinburgh University Press 1998) 138–139.)

15 Gilles Deleuze, *Cinema 2*, (Continuum, 2005), xiii.

16 Deleuze, "Doubts About the Imaginary," 66.

17 Ibid.

18 "It might also be urged that what is difficult and enforced is incompatible with blessedness; if the movement of the soul is not of its essence, movement of the soul must be contrary to its nature. It must also be painful for the soul to be inextricably bound up with the body; nay more, if, as is frequently said and widely accepted, it is better for mind not to be embodied, the union must be for it undesirable." (See: Aristotle, *On the Soul (De Anima)*,

translated by J.A. Smith (The Internet Classics Archive), http://classics.mit.edu/Aristotle/soul.1.i.html)

19 Friedrich Nietzsche, *Human, All Too Human*, (The Project Gutenberg Ebook), https://www.gutenberg.org/files/38145/38145-h/38145-h.htm

20 Gilles Deleuze, "To Have Done with Judgment," *Essays Clinical and Critical*, (University of Minnesota Press 1997), 130.

21 Ibid.

22 In Deleuze's *The Logic of Sense*, he discusses the problematic of surface and depth throughout an appendix section entitled "Phantasm and Modern Literature" under the subheading "Michel Tournier and the World Without Others."

23 Félix Guattari, *Soft Subversions: Texts and Interviews 1977–1985*, (Semiotext(e) 2009), 184.

24 François Laruelle, "Non-Philosophy as Heresy," *From Decision to Heresy: Experiments in Non-Standard Thought*, translated by Taylor Adkins, (Urbanomic 2012), 261.

25 Gerald Raunig, *Dividuum*, (Semiotext(e) 2016), 25–36.

26 Friedrich Nietzsche, *Human, All Too Human*, (T.N. Foulis 1910), 75.

27 Ibid.

28 Klaus Theleweit, *Male Fantasies, Volume 1: Women, Floods, Bodies, History (Theory and History of Literature, Volume 22)*, (University of Minnesota Press 1987).

29 James Hillman, *A Blue Fire*, (Harper Perennial, 1989), 82

30 Ibid.

31 C.G. Jung, *Memories, Dreams, Reflections*, (Vintage Books; Reissue edition 1989), 197.

32 Deleuze and Guattari, *A Thousand Plateaus*, 33.

33 C.G. Jung, *Collected Works* 13, paragraph 18.

34 Gilles Deleuze, "From Sacher-Masoch to Masochism," *Angelaki: Journal of the Theoretical Humanities*, Volume 9, (2004), translated by Christian Kerslake.

35 James Hillman, "Psychology: Monotheistic or Polytheistic?" in: *Working with Images*, edited by Benjamin Sells, (Spring Publications, 2000), 22–24.

36 Ibid., 21.

37 Ibid., 29.

38 C.G. Jung, *Psychological Types*, (Bollingen, 1971), 318.

39 Hillman, "Psychology: Monotheistic or Polytheistic?," 39.

40 Ibid.

41 Jay Conway, *Gilles Deleuze: Affirmation in Philosophy*, (Palgrave Macmillan, 2010), 101.

42 Stanton Marlan, *The Black Sun: The Alchemy and Art of Darkness*, (Texas A&M, 2005), 167.

43 Ibid.

44 James Hillman, *A Blue Fire*, narrated by James Hillman (BetterListen, 2012).

45 Ibid.

46 Ibid.

47 James Hillman, "Persons as Types," *From Types to Images: Uniform Edition Vol. 4*, (Spring Publications 2018), 39.

48 Ibid.

49 James Hillman, "Egalitarian Typologies Versus The Perception of the Unique," http://www.compilerpress.ca/Competitiveness/Anno/Anno%20Hillman%20Egal%201.htm

50 Gaston Bachelard, *The Psychoanalysis of Fire*, (Quartet Encounters, 1964), 110.

51 Hillman, *A Blue Fire*, 74.

52 James Hillman, "The Context of Soul-Making," *From Types to Images: Uniform Edition, Vol. 4*, (Spring Publications, 2018), 83.

53 "The psyche wants to find itself by seeing through; even more, it loves to be enlightened by seeing through itself, as if the very act of seeing through clarified and made the soul transparent — as if psychologizing with ideas were itself an archetypal therapy, enlightening, illuminating." (See: Hillman, *A Blue Fire*, 55.)

54 Mary Watkins, "Breaking the Vessels: Archetypal Psychology and the Restoration of Culture, Community, and Ecology," https://www.mary-watkins.net/wp-content/uploads/2019/05/Breaking-the-Vessels.pdf, 22.

55 Ibid., 239.

56 Ibid., 238.

57 Deleuze and Guattari, *A Thousand Plateaus*, 279–294.

CONCLUDING UN-CYBERNETIC POSTSCRIPT: WHAT IS PHILOSOPHY?

1 Giorgio Agamben, *The Church and the Kingdom*, (Seagull Books, 2018), 41.

ACKNOWLEDGEMENTS

This book wouldn't have been possible without the support, faith, and feedback of our families, nor would it have ever become an actuality without the help of our comrades Carl, Tariq, Josh, our proofreader Matt, and everybody at Repeater Books and Zer0.

Massive thanks to our co-conspirator Noah Trapolino for his illustrations, assistance, and acephalic *nous*. We also want to thank Matt, Jigme, Violet, Terry, Archie, and Billie, for reading over some of the key sections of this book without which it would've truly suffered.

Of course, we cannot say less than that we have unending gratitude for our listeners, viewers, and supporters. For their years of comradeship and collectivity, be it in reading groups, live shows, or amongst the flows of cyberspace.

REPEATER BOOKS

is dedicated to the creation of a new reality. The landscape of twenty-first-century arts and letters is faded and inert, riven by fashionable cynicism, egotistical self-reference and a nostalgia for the recent past. Repeater intends to add its voice to those movements that wish to enter history and assert control over its currents, gathering together scattered and isolated voices with those who have already called for an escape from Capitalist Realism. Our desire is to publish in every sphere and genre, combining vigorous dissent and a pragmatic willingness to succeed where messianic abstraction and quiescent co-option have stalled: abstention is not an option: we are alive and we don't agree.